ZUMBA® LOVERS COOKBOOK

favorite recipes & success stories from fans around the world

ASHLEY POUND, EDITOR

PUBLISHED BY ZUMBA FITNESS

ZUMBA® fitness

Copyright © 2012 by Zumba Fitness, LLC

Editor & Publisher: Ashley Pound
Nutrition Advisers: Molly Morgan, RD, CDN, CSSD, and Anastasia Conover, MS, RD, CDN, CNSC

Content was solicited and produced by Ashley Pound Creative for Zumba Fitness and includes recipes from Zumba® lovers around the world. Selected recipes were formatted, modified and tested by Jorj Morgan, Anastasia Conover, Anna Berman, Janine M. Koutsky and the editor. Nutrition facts were reviewed for accuracy by registered dietitians Molly Morgan and Anastasia Conover.

Interviews conducted by Lauren Somers and Susannah Felts

Food photography by Francesco Tonelli | Zumba® community photography by Juliet Cannici
Personal photos submitted by recipe authors and reproduced with their permission
Food styling by Simon Andrews | Prop styling by Lynn Tonelli | Props provided by ABC Homes and Jono Pandolfi

Creative direction by Hilary Fitch | Design by Sarah Rusin | Page production and indexing by Ashley Pound

Note: Each recipe contributor has agreed to a release stating that the submitted recipe is his or her original work. Any similarity to other published works is unintended. While changes or additions may have been made to a recipe to conform to the cookbook's nutrition or style guidelines, every effort has been made to honor the integrity of the original. For recipes with significant changes, we note that they are inspired by the contributors' recipes.

This cookbook contains recipes and nutritional information and is intended for educational purposes only. While tips and ingredient substitutions have been added to accommodate a wide variety of reader preferences, the content does not conform to a specific health, wellness or diet plan and should not be treated as such. Information in this book offers no guarantees on the part of the editor or publishers nor is it a substitute for professional medical or dietetic advice. If you or a member of your family has any disease or health condition that is or could be related to or affected by your diet, you should consult with a medical or dietetic professional before using any of these recipes or nutritional information. The editor and publishers disclaim all liability in connection with the use of this book and are not responsible for any injury or other loss that allegedly results either directly or indirectly from the use of the recipes or nutritional information in this book. Nor are the editor and publishers responsible for allergic or other adverse reactions or effects that allegedly result from eating these dishes. Your use of all recipes and nutritional information in this book is solely at your own risk. Recipes and claims made by contributors here reflect their personal tastes, philosophies and experiences and in no way represent the policies or opinions of Zumba Fitness, LLC, Ashley Pound Creative LLC or Zumba® instructors.

Published by Zumba Fitness, LLC, Hallandale, Florida, USA

First Edition 2012

10 9 8 7 6 5 4 3 2 1

Publisher's Cataloging-in-Publication data

Zumba lovers cookbook : favorite recipes & success stories from fans around the world / Ashley Pound, editor.
   p. cm.
   ISBN 978-0-615-72178-1
   Includes biographical references and index.
1. International cooking. 2. Cookbooks. I. Zumba lovers cookbook : favorite recipes and success stories from fans around the world. II. Pound, Ashley.

TX742 .Z86 2012
641.5/637—dc23
                              2012916897

Manufactured in the United States

In the United States, ZUMBA®, ZUMBA FITNESS®, ZUMBATHON®, ZUMBAWEAR®, ZLIFE® and Z-LIFE™ are trademarks of Zumba Fitness, LLC. As of this publication date, Zumba Fitness, LLC, owns trademark registrations in many countries, including all members of the European Community, most of North and South America, Asia and Oceania, and has filed for variations of Zumba® trademarks worldwide.

CONNECT WITH US: ZUMBA.COM, ZUMBAFITNESSGAME.COM, ZLIFE.ZUMBA.COM 🅣 @ZUMBA 🅣 @ZLIFEMAG 🅕 ZUMBA 🅕 ZLIFEMAG

DEDICATED TO ZUMBA® LOVERS EVERYWHERE

This cookbook is dedicated to the 14 million Zumba Fitness® fans who see life as a celebration. The joy and energy you bring to the dance floor, to our online Zumba community and to people in need through charity Zumbathons® have made this dance-fitness phenomenon a force for health and happiness worldwide. We hope the recipes and stories shared here by fellow Zumba lovers will make your experience even richer.

CONTENTS

COOKBOOK KEY

Ⅴ VEGETARIAN (OVO-LACTO) DISHES
For definitions of "vegetarian" and "vegan," see page 152. For tips on converting meat dishes to meatless ones, see recipe pages and the "Glossary & Substitutions" section, page 145.

🌶 SPICY DISHES
Dishes have been identified as spicy or not by their contributors. See recipe pages for tips on adjusting the level of heat in spicy dishes.

Healthy eating requires awareness and balance. We've rated these dishes to help you plan meals. You're welcome!

★★★ ZUMBA ALL-STARS
Our top picks for health-conscious cooks!

★★ OCCASIONAL EATS
Yummy dishes with an ingredient or two that should be used in moderation. Try our suggested substitutes to make them all-stars.

★ SOMETIME SPLURGES
Rich dishes for the occasional indulgence.

[Z] ZUMBA FIT TIPS
For official Zumba Fitness substitutions, look for the pink "Z"!

FOREWORD

As the editor-in-chief of SHAPE®, a magazine devoted to helping women achieve their goals and live a healthy lifestyle, I've seen firsthand the positive impact that Zumba Fitness® has had on virtually everyone who's ever taken a class. The movement has dramatically changed so many of our readers' lives. Each day, we receive letters from Zumba enthusiasts sharing their personal stories of triumph. From shedding pounds and inches to changing their outlook on life for the better, thousands of readers credit Zumba Fitness with their success. For this reason, SHAPE has developed a strong partnership with the movement through events, programs and more.

You simply cannot deny the power of this global fitness phenomenon and the amazing effect it has on people's lives. To its fans, Zumba Fitness is not simply a form of exercise but a celebration of life. No wonder SHAPE wants to share in the excitement!

With this cookbook, Zumba lovers have yet another resource—recipes for delicious dishes that are good for you and fun to make—to help you achieve your healthy goals. These dishes have been created by enthusiasts around the world who approach cooking the same way they approach exercise—with a sense of joy and adventure and a stay-fit mindset. And talk about motivation! Many recipes are accompanied by the contributors' personal stories of how Zumba Fitness has helped them lose weight and create a healthier lifestyle.

Thanks to Zumba Fitness, torching calories has never been so enjoyable. And now the same can be said about eating healthy. So come on ... get shakin' across the dance floor—and in the kitchen!

Tara Kraft, Editor-in-Chief

SHAPE®

INTRODUCTION

Walk by a Zumba Fitness class, and you can feel the heat. Walls pulse, fists pump, hips sway and the dancers are so on fire, they steam up the windows! All that energy makes you wonder what they've been eating for breakfast—or lunch or dinner. After all, a raucous crew like this would never settle for bland and boring in the kitchen.

To find out what's cooking, we invited fellow Zumba lovers to share their favorite recipes, healthy-eating tips and personal fitness stories. And what a response! Submissions came from around the world—Auckland, Buenos Aires, New York, Toronto and all parts in between. The dishes are as diverse as their creators—from Thai Beef Salad to Eggplant Hummus to King Prawn Chili Pasta—and reflect a variety of tastes, styles and eating philosophies. The result? A global community cookbook to feed your Zumba fire!

A LOVE AFFAIR WITH FOOD & FITNESS

Some of our selected contributors are Zumba instructors; others are students. Some are trained chefs and registered dietitians; others are home cooks. All share an enthusiasm for fitness and food, as you'll see in their stories throughout the book. What we love about these contributors is what we love about our whole Zumba family: They add their own special flavor to everything they do—on and off the dance floor. See the "Glossary & Substitutions" section (page 145) for info about the foods featured in these dishes and alternate ingredients to give them your own special touches.

IS THIS A DIET BOOK?

No, these recipes were not created by Zumba Fitness and are not part of an official diet plan. This book is by and for Zumba lovers—a fun and informative resource to enhance your Zumba lifestyle. While there are plenty of lean dishes in the mix, there are also rich ones for the occasional splurge. We encourage you to team up with a qualified nutrition adviser to determine your needs and adapt these recipes to your nutrition goals—just as you might consult a fitness adviser to help set your fitness goals.

Some of the recipes tested have been modified to conform to a few nutritional guidelines or to include more accessible ingredients, but we've maintained the integrity of the originals and included plenty of tips to help you adapt the recipes to your personal needs. If you want to reduce saturated fat, we tell you how. If you're vegetarian, we offer tips to make dishes meatless. If you're exploring flavors from other cultures, we give you lots of enticing options.

HEALTHY EATING IS NOT "ONE SIZE FITS ALL"

That's what's so fascinating about food and nutrition! What we eat depends on so many factors—our heritage, personal taste, health condition, activity level and the availability and cost of foods. Some of you might be tackling a weight problem, like Janine Hawthorne (page 22), or cross-training for a marathon, like John Stack (page 23), or eating for two, like Liz Gannon (page 107). What's right for one person isn't always right for another. But despite the different needs and desires of the Zumba lovers featured in this book, they all seem to share a few common-sense beliefs about healthy eating:

Enjoy it or you won't stick with it. Boring diets—just like boring workouts—rarely inspire commitment.

Label-reading rocks! When you check the nutrition facts, you make healthier choices. Period.

Cooking is empowering. If you make your own meals, you know what's really fueling that fabulous body of yours!

Exploration excites the senses. Try dishes from other countries, cultures or cooking styles to bust out of a food rut. Experiment with new ingredients and flavors, and you just may discover a new favorite.

TO THRIVE, DON'T DEPRIVE

Food is one of life's great pleasures, but many of us equate pleasure with things that are bad for us. Why should healthy eating and tasty food be mutually exclusive? As one Zumba fan put it, *(Continued page 14)*

INTRODUCTION (CONTINUED)

"I wasn't going to stop eating what I loved, but I wanted the most bang for my exercise buck." So she started eating her favorite foods in moderation, paying more attention to the quality of the ingredients, savoring the flavors and enjoying sweets as occasional—rather than everyday—treats. The recipe contributors here show us that eating "right" can mean eating well. It's about pampering your body—not denying it.

Molly Morgan, RD, CDN, CSSD, nutrition consultant to this cookbook and author of *The Skinny Rules: The 101 Secrets Every Skinny Girl Knows*, offers a few suggestions.

Focus on nutrient-rich dishes. If you're looking to lose weight, your natural reaction may be to start skipping meals to cut calories. That's not the most effective way to move the scale in the right direction. Food is fuel for your body, and you need lots of nutrients to keep it healthy and strong.

Focus on getting most of your calories from high-quality foods and minimize "empty" calories such as those from white sugar and processed snacks. To decide how many calories you need per day, check out free calorie-estimation tools and weight-loss information at choosemyplate.gov.

Set realistic goals. A reasonable rate for weight loss is 1 to 2 pounds per week. If weight loss is your aim, work with your health-care provider or a registered dietitian to establish goals you can sustain.

How much *you eat* is just as important as *what you eat*. Even an extra 50 calories per day can add up to 5 extra pounds over the course of a year. Portion control is key. The nutrition facts offered at the end of each recipe in this book are calculated per serving. Check the number of portions in a dish to be aware of the actual number of calories you're eating in a meal.

Take it easy on your body. If you eat too much at one meal, it can be difficult for your body to properly digest the food—or benefit from its nutrients. Spacing out your mealtimes and snack times over the course of a day can help with digestion and maximize your body's absorption of nutrients. It can also help keep your hunger in check.

Take care of your heart. Reducing saturated fat and eliminating trans fat—linked to an increase in LDL blood cholesterol (the bad stuff)—help maintain heart health.

To find dishes with low saturated fat, check product labels and the nutrition facts accompanying these recipes. Trans fat is primarily found in processed foods, including commercially prepared baked goods, snacks and fried foods. The U.S. Food and Drug Administration allows up to half a gram of trans fat per serving in products labeled "trans-fat free." To eliminate this unhealthy fat from your diet, avoid eating any product with "hydrogenated oil"—the source of trans fat—listed on the ingredients label.

Focusing your diet on lean protein sources—such as trimmed flank steak, skinless chicken breast, low-fat milk, reduced-fat cheeses and certain beans and legumes—also helps control LDL levels. So does increasing your fiber intake. When selecting breads, cereals and grains, choose whole-grain varieties, which retain more fiber and nutrients. You can also get fiber from vegetables, fruits, beans and legumes. Sources include almonds, apples, berries, broccoli, chickpeas, kale, lima beans and peas.

How much fiber do you need? Aim for at least 25 to 30 grams of fiber a day. When you increase your fiber intake, drink more fluids to help fiber do its job.

Have a little salt sense. Hypertension (high blood pressure) can lead to heart failure, kidney failure or stroke, and among the risk factors are stress, a sedentary lifestyle and too much salt in your diet. The good news: If you're taking Zumba classes a few times a week, you're already fending off the first two risks! But if salt is your go-to seasoning—or you eat lots of high-sodium processed foods—it's time for a change. These recipes offer a wealth of flavors to expand your palate, and while the dishes are not all low-sodium, cooking them yourself lets you control just how much salt goes into your meals.

Get sweet on healthy foods. With so much added and "hidden" sugar in bottled drinks, grab-and-go snacks, breads, cereals and other prepackaged foods, sugar overload can be tough to avoid—and the truth is, many of us don't try. As a society, we love our convenience foods and often ignore all the startling news reports that warn about sugar's role in obesity, Type 2 diabetes, heart stress, liver toxicity and other threatening conditions. Some health pros liken sugar to alcohol, tobacco and other addictive substances! What's a Zumba lover with a sweet tooth to do?

Choose quality over quantity. Instead of mindlessly grabbing a chocolate "health" bar every time you're in a checkout line, resolve to eat sweets more mindfully. Adapt a favorite dessert with more healthful ingredients such as date paste *(see "Great Dates," page 116)* or fresh fruit. Bake a cake from scratch and invite friends to share, so you won't overeat. Bank calories for a special treat by cutting back on processed foods or using the occasional no-calorie sweetener. If you're aiming to eliminate sugar altogether, start by cutting a recipe's sugar in half to get used to less sweetness and to appreciate the other flavors in the dish *(see "Sugar & Substitutes, page 149).*

THINK LIKE AN ATHLETE

Thinking of food as fuel is valuable for everyone, but for active Zumba fans—and athletes as a group—it's essential. The type of food and fluids you choose can have a real impact on your workout experience.

Before a workout. Knowing what and when to eat before exercise is important. For most people, a light snack or "mini-meal" one hour before exercise is ideal. That gives your body time to digest the food and provide energy for optimal performance.

Aim for a snack that's made up primarily of carbohydrates and some protein but little fat. Foods with high fat content—even healthy fats—can take too long to digest, sitting in your system and causing indigestion during a workout. Drink at least 16 ounces of water, too. If you have special pre-workout needs, like Charise Richards *(page 104)*, you'll want to discuss options with your doctor.

During a workout. For workouts lasting one hour or less, sip 4 to 6 ounces of water every 15 to 20 minutes, for a total of 16 to 24 ounces. If your workout will be longer than an hour, consider adding a high-carb sports drink. Why? The body oxidizes about 30 to 60 grams of carbs per hour of exercise, so upping your carb intake for longer sessions helps with endurance and performance.

After a workout. After a Zumba session, your body needs to refuel, repair and recover in preparation for your next workout, and this is true even if you are trying to lose weight. Eat a 3-to-1 ratio of carbs to protein, and drink 16 to 24 ounces of water. The carbs refuel the stores in your muscles, and the protein helps repair and build muscle. Protein can even help carbs reach muscles more easily.

NOTES ABOUT THE RECIPES IN THIS BOOK

Ingredients. For submitted recipes using specialty ingredients or foods that are unique to a certain region of the world, we've provided definitions and suggested resources—or replaced those foods with more universally available ingredients.

Nutrition facts. Unquantified ingredients or ingredients labeled "optional" are intended to be used at your discretion and are not factored into the nutrition information at the end of each recipe. For example, if a recipe calls for salt without a specified measure, any salt you add will increase the sodium noted in the nutrition facts.

Prep/cook time. The total estimated time for ingredient preparation and cooking or baking is included with each recipe. Separate estimates for time needed—unattended—to marinate, freeze, dry or slow-cook food are added to help you plan your meals.

Conversions. All recipes use U.S. measurements. See "Metric Conversions" *(page 152)* for tips on converting to metric measurements. Note that these are estimates only.

Brand names. Specific brand names for unusual or hard-to-find products are offered as a service to readers and are not endorsed by or connected with Zumba Fitness in any way.

Substitutions. The recipes selected were chosen for their exciting mix of foods and flavors—a reflection of our diverse Zumba community. As a group, the recipes do not reflect a particular dietary discipline—such as "clean" eating, macrobiotic, vegetarian, diabetic—nor do they represent an official weight-management system. We encourage you to adapt the dishes to your personal dietary needs using tips on the recipe pages and in the "Glossary & Substitutions" section *(page 145).*

Recipes were not tested with these substitutions. If you try them, write to editorial@zlifemag.com and let us know how they've worked for you. We're eager to share your recommendations and results with fellow Zumba lovers!

— EDITOR

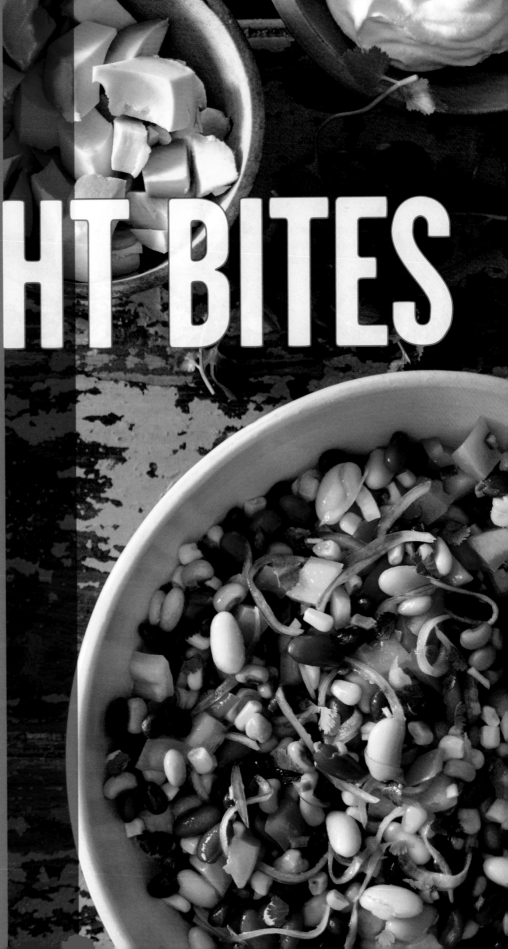

LIGHT BITES

SNACKS & FINGER FOODS

Skip empty-calorie munchies and go for nutritious snacks like the ones on these pages. You can jump-start your day—or your workout—with Tangy Apple Cheese Toast (*page 19*), bubbling from the broiler. At work, bypass junk-food vending machines and reach for chopped veggies dipped in Classic Hummus (*page 23*)—easy to store in the office fridge. For buffets or parties, mix up a batch of Holiday Cocktail Meatballs (*page 22*)—small bites with big flavor. Most of these dishes can be prepped ahead and assembled or cooked before serving, so you'll always have a filling snack or party pleaser at the ready!

★★★ **ZUMBA ALL-STARS**
★★☆ **OCCASIONAL EATS**
★☆☆ **SOMETIME SPLURGES**

MANGO-PEACH SALSA

FROM DEBORAH MANDZUK OF ALBERTA, CANADA

SCOOP UP THIS FRUITY DIP WITH CELERY STICKS, ZUCCHINI SLICES AND RED PEPPERS—OR TRY IT AS A FILLING FOR STUFFED MUSHROOMS.

MAKES 2 SERVINGS | TOTAL PREP TIME: 10 MINUTES PLUS 30 MINUTES FOR FLAVORS TO MELD **V**

★★★

INGREDIENTS

· 1 medium ripe mango, peeled, pitted, diced (about 1 cup)
· 2 medium ripe peaches, peeled, pitted, diced (about 1 cup)
· ¼ medium white onion, peeled, chopped (about ¼ cup)
· ¼ cup chopped fresh cilantro
· 1 large jalapeño pepper, seeded, deveined, diced (about 2 tablespoons)
· 1 large lime, juiced (about 2 tablespoons)
· Coarse salt and freshly ground pepper

DIRECTIONS

Combine all of the ingredients in a bowl. Cover with plastic wrap and let stand for 30 minutes so that the flavors meld.

....

Per serving 104 calories, 0 grams total fat, 0 grams saturated fat, 0 grams monounsaturated fat, 0 grams polyunsaturated fat, 0 milligrams cholesterol, 27 grams carbohydrates, 4 grams fiber, 1 gram protein, 3 milligrams sodium

➜ DRESSED-UP DISH

Sweet and spicy salsas can add zing to main dishes, too! For a light entrée, spoon salsa over grilled chicken, fish or tofu. Or try it over shredded zucchini "noodles" for a raw-food option.

DEBORAH'S STORY
RAW ENERGY

As a dancer and Zumba instructor, I've always been active, but my diet was causing blood-sugar highs and lows and digestion problems that affected my mood and energy. And two hours after a meal, I'd be hungry again, so I never felt satisfied.

Then I went to a raw-food weekend retreat and discovered an eating style that works great for me. Here's what makes me feel amazing every day:

A good start. For breakfast, I go for a fruit salad with soaked nuts and seeds or a green fruit smoothie. I eat until I feel satisfied.

Good timing. My largest meal of the day is midafternoon, when I load up on whatever greens I have on hand—spinach, lettuce, kale, collards, chard or parsley. Adding veggies, nuts, seeds and, occasionally, sprouted grains makes for a filling lunch.

After Zumba classes, I always have a snack but avoid eating less than two hours before bedtime. This way, my body isn't digesting food when I'm trying to sleep.

Great perks. While I haven't gone 100 percent raw, I believe I've reaped real benefits from incorporating more raw food into my diet. I feel satisfied for longer stretches of time; my digestion has improved; my immunity to illness seems stronger and I have fewer mood swings and more energy. To top it off, my skin looks radiant!

TANGY APPLE CHEESE TOAST
FROM LIANA YATES OF BRITISH COLUMBIA, CANADA

MAKE THIS HIGH-PROTEIN SPREAD FOR BREAKFAST OR AS AN AFTERNOON TREAT.

MAKES 1 SERVING | TOTAL PREP/COOK TIME: 10 MINUTES **V**
★ ★ ☆

INGREDIENTS
- 1 slice crusty, whole-grain bread
- ⅓ Granny Smith apple, peeled, cored, shredded or cut into matchsticks (about ⅓ cup)
- ¼ cup low-fat (1% milk fat) cottage cheese, drained
- ¼ teaspoon natural brown sugar (or more to taste)
- ¼ teaspoon apple pie spice (or substitute ground cinnamon or ginger)

DIRECTIONS
Toast the bread lightly and place it in a baking dish. Heat the oven on the broil setting. Mix together the apple and cottage cheese in a small bowl. Stir in the sugar. Spread the mixture onto the toasted bread. Sprinkle with apple pie spice. Broil in the oven until warm and bubbly, about 1 to 3 minutes, watching constantly to prevent burning.

....

Per serving 140 calories, 1.5 grams total fat, .5 gram saturated fat, .5 gram monounsaturated fat, 0 grams polyunsaturated fat, 2 milligrams cholesterol, 21 grams carbohydrates, 3 grams fiber, 11 grams protein, 364 milligrams sodium

[Z] Substitute ½ teaspoon Stevia in the Raw® (or favorite no-calorie sweetener). *See "Stevia 411," page 119, for more info.*

➜ **BETTER BREAD**
Find healthy whole-grain breads sold in your area: Go to wholegrainscouncil.org/find-whole-grains/breads.

➜ **GET EXTRA FIBER**
Leave the peel on the apple and shred in a food processor.

CAPRESE CROSTINI

FROM ANNE HERNANDEZ OF FLORIDA, USA

WHAT A LOVELY START TO A LIGHT SUMMER MEAL!
MAKES 6 SERVINGS | *TOTAL PREP/COOK TIME: 15 MINUTES* **V**
★ ★ ☆

INGREDIENTS
· 3-4 large Roma tomatoes, cut into ¼-inch slices
· Coarse salt and freshly ground pepper
· 1 (8-ounce) loaf French-style whole-grain bread
· 8 ounces fresh mozzarella cheese, cut into thin slices
· Balsamic vinegar

DIRECTIONS
Preheat the oven to 400°. Season the tomato slices with salt and pepper.

Cut the bread into ½-inch diagonal slices. Arrange on a baking sheet and spray both sides of the bread with vegetable oil spray. Bake until the bread is golden on one side. Turn the bread and bake until golden on the other side, about 3 minutes more. Remove from the oven.

Divide the mozzarella and tomato slices evenly to top each slice of bread. Return to the oven and bake until the cheese melts, about 3 minutes more. Remove from the oven and transfer to a platter. Lightly drizzle each crostini with balsamic vinegar.

....

Per serving 241 calories, 11 grams total fat, 6 grams saturated fat, 3 grams monounsaturated fat, 1 gram polyunsaturated fat, 34 milligrams cholesterol, 24 grams total carbohydrates, 2 grams fiber, 12 grams protein, 394 milligrams sodium

ANNE'S STORY
GETTING HER GROOVE BACK

For much of my life, I had been
active and trim—a dancer in a
Celtic troupe. But over time,
life's stresses led to lifestyle
changes, and I started packing
on the pounds. When I reached
222, I decided enough was
enough. I wanted to be healthier—
and I wanted my husband
to look at me the way he had
when we first met.

The more the merrier. We started
eating a Mediterranean-inspired
diet and taking Zumba classes
together. Seeing my enthusiasm
and the changes in my figure,
my co-workers started coming
to class, too. Soon, our company
was offering classes at the office!

Making progress. I've lost
40 pounds so far and am on my
way to losing another 40!
More important, I'm happier and
have more energy—and it's
nice to see that twinkle in my
husband's eye again.

→ **PERSONAL TOUCH**
*Garnish with
your favorite
fresh herb, such
as basil, for
an additional
flavor boost!*

HEATING OIL

➤ **Pros & cons.** Cooking with oil can impart flavor, enhance texture and, in the case of some oils, provide a few healthful nutrients. Good-quality olive oil, for example, may offer antioxidant and anti-inflammatory nutrients and is high in the monounsaturated fats that may help raise HDL (good) cholesterol. But like all cooking oils, it also adds calories and fat to a dish—which puts it in the use-with-discretion category—and it can be harmful to your health if cooked above its smoke point.

➤ **Why you should care.** Heating oil above its smoke point (the temperature at which the oil begins to smoke) can degrade the oil's nutrients and flavor. It may also pro-duce free radicals that can contrib-ute to the risk of cancer. Additional health concerns are being studied.

Here's a list of smoke points and the maximum flame over which oils should be heated. Because olive oil companies report dramatically different smoke points for their extra-virgin brands (250°-400°), err on the side of safety and use this heart-healthy oil cold or cooked at up to medium heat.

STOVETOP SETTINGS: MEDIUM (M), MEDIUM-HIGH (MH), HIGH (H)

OIL TYPE	MAX FLAME	APPROX. SMOKE POINT
EXTRA-VIRGIN OLIVE	M	325°
CANOLA (SEMIREFINED)	MH	350°
COCONUT	MH	350°
PURE OLIVE (2% ACIDITY)	H	420°
SESAME (SEMIREFINED)	H	450°
EXTRA-LIGHT OLIVE (HIGHLY REFINED)	H	468°

For more info on oils and fats—as well as suggestions for cooking without them—see "Butter & Substitutes," page 145, and "Oils, Fats & Substitutes," page 148.

HOLIDAY COCKTAIL MEATBALLS

FROM JANINE HAWTHORNE OF NEW YORK, USA

HAVING A LITTLE SOIRÉE TO CELEBRATE THE SEASON? THIS IS PERFECT PARTY FOOD.

MAKES 6 SERVINGS | TOTAL PREP/COOK TIME: 45 MINUTES
★ ★ ★

INGREDIENTS

· 1 tablespoon olive oil
· ⅓ medium white onion, peeled, chopped (about ⅓ cup)
· 1 medium celery rib, diced (about ⅓ cup)
· ⅓ cup dried cranberries
· ½ cup homemade or prepared low-sodium chicken broth
· 1 pound lean ground turkey
· ⅓ cup whole-grain bread crumbs
· ½-1 teaspoon poultry seasoning
· Coarse salt and freshly ground pepper

DIRECTIONS

Preheat the oven to 350°. Coat a baking sheet with a lip in vegetable oil spray. Heat the oil in a skillet over medium heat. Cook the onion and celery until soft, about 5 minutes. Add the dried cranberries and pour in the broth. Cook until all liquid is absorbed, about 6 minutes more. Remove the pan from the heat and cool to room temperature.

Place the ground turkey, bread crumbs and poultry seasoning into a large bowl. Season with salt and pepper. Add the cranberries and vegetables. Use your hands to combine all of the ingredients. Shape into 24 (1½-inch) balls. Place the meatballs onto the baking sheet and bake until they are cooked through, about 20 to 25 minutes. For parties, serve the meat-balls warm on a platter, with toothpicks for spearing.

....

Per serving 156 calories, 8 grams total fat, 2 grams saturated fat, 3.5 grams monounsaturated fat, 1.5 grams polyunsaturated fat, 49 milligrams cholesterol, 10 grams carbohydrates, .5 gram fiber, 11 grams protein, 83 milligrams sodium

JANINE'S STORY
BORN TO BE FABULOUS

I went from 325 to 225 pounds with gastric bypass surgery—and then the weight stopped coming off. It took Zumba classes and eating better-quality foods to get down to a size 10—and I'm still losing!

Here are four nutrition guidelines I now live by:

1. Drink up! Before every meal, I drink 20 ounces of water. This aids digestion, keeps me hydrated, fills my stomach and is great for the skin.

2. Get real. I go for whole, fresh, "real" foods.

3. Cave in to a crave. If I always deny myself the things I love—like an occasional slice or two of pizza—I feel unsatisfied and overeat later.

4. Be a super eater. I eat from the "superfoods" list every day—mostly spinach, tomatoes, turkey, Greek yogurt, blueberries and walnuts. The nutritional value is intense!

After learning to eat well and dancing my way into great shape, I trained to become a Zumba instructor and found I had all this energy and creativity to share with my students. I feel I'm finally who I was born to be!

CLASSIC HUMMUS
FROM JOHN STACK OF WISCONSIN, USA

AS AN APPETIZER OR SNACK, THIS MEDITERRANEAN FAVORITE PACKS A LOT OF FLAVOR IN A FEW BITES.
MAKES 8 SERVINGS | TOTAL PREP TIME: 15 MINUTES **V**
★★★

INGREDIENTS
· 1 (14.5-ounce) can chickpeas, drained
· 4 tablespoons natural, unsweetened applesauce
· 1 medium lemon, juiced (about 3 tablespoons)
· 2 tablespoons tahini (or substitute with smooth peanut butter)
· 1 teaspoon ground cumin
· 1 teaspoon ground coriander
· 1 medium garlic clove, peeled, minced (about 1 teaspoon)
· ½ teaspoon crushed red pepper flakes
· ½ teaspoon onion powder
· ½ teaspoon celery seed
· 1 (14-ounce) can pitted, sliced black olives, drained

DIRECTIONS
Place all of the ingredients into the bowl of a food processor fitted with a steel blade. Pulse to combine. Season with salt and pepper. Hummus should be the consistency of smooth guacamole. For the best flavor, store the hummus in an airtight container and refrigerate overnight. For dipping into the hummus, use grilled pita bread, tortilla chips, sliced cucumbers, carrot sticks or red pepper slices.

....

Per serving 91 calories, 3 grams total fat, 0 grams saturated fat, 1 gram monounsaturated fat, 1 gram polyunsaturated fat, 0 milligrams cholesterol, 14 grams carbohydrates, 3 grams fiber, 3 grams protein, 276 milligrams sodium

"I look at the nutrition content on prepackaged foods and think, I can beat that, easy!" —JOHN

➔ HEART SMART

While this snack is higher in fat than some others, most of the fat here comes from heart-healthy olive oil. Opt for extra-virgin oil, the most nutrient-rich variety made from the first press of the olive.

EGGPLANT HUMMUS

FROM NANCY PILARSKI OF INDIANA, USA

ENJOY THIS VEGGIE DIP WITH WEDGES OF PITA, CRACKERS, WHOLE-GRAIN CROSTINI OR CELERY AND CARROT STICKS.

MAKES 6 SERVINGS | *TOTAL PREP/COOK TIME: 45 MINUTES* **V**
★ ★ ★

INGREDIENTS
· 1 (1-pound) eggplant, peeled, cut into 2-inch pieces (about 4 cups)
· 2 tablespoons extra-light olive oil *(see "Heating Oil," page 22)*
· ⅓ cup extra-virgin olive oil
· Coarse salt and freshly ground pepper
· 1 (15.5-ounce) can chickpeas, drained
· 1 medium lemon, juiced (about 3 tablespoons)
· ⅓ cup chopped fresh parsley
· 1 medium garlic clove, peeled, minced (about 1 teaspoon)

DIRECTIONS
Preheat the oven to 450°. Place the eggplant onto a baking sheet with a lip. Drizzle with 2 tablespoons extra-light olive oil, and season with salt and pepper. Bake until the eggplant is soft, about 20 to 25 minutes. Cool to room temperature.

Place the chickpeas, lemon juice, parsley, garlic and eggplant into the bowl of a food processor. Pulse to combine. With the machine running, slowly pour in the ⅓ cup extra-virgin olive oil. Season with salt and pepper.

· ·

Per serving 253 calories, 17 grams total fat, 2 grams saturated fat, 12 grams monounsaturated fat, 2 grams polyunsaturated fat, 0 milligrams cholesterol, 21 grams carbohydrates, 5 grams fiber, 4 grams protein, 223 milligrams sodium

➡ **DIPPIN' CHIPS**
For a satisfying crunch, cut whole-wheat or multigrain pita into triangles. Brush with extra-light olive oil (optional) and spread the pieces in a single layer on a middle rack in the oven. Bake 6 minutes at 425° or until crisp and golden. Sprinkle with coarse salt if desired.

MINI BEAN TACOS

APRIL CRISOSTOMO OF ARIZONA, USA

***THROWING A ZUMBA VIDEO GAME PARTY? SERVE UP THIS
COLORFUL DISH—BUFFET STYLE—AFTER THE COOL DOWN.***

*MAKES 24 SERVINGS | TOTAL PREP/COOK TIME: 20 MINUTES
PLUS 8 HOURS TO MARINATE* V 🌶

★★☆

INGREDIENTS

· ½ cup natural granulated sugar ————————
· ¾ cup canola oil
· 1 cup apple cider vinegar
· 1 (15.5-ounce) can black beans, drained, rinsed
· 1 (15.5-ounce) can white beans, drained, rinsed
· 1 (15.5-ounce) can red beans, drained, rinsed
· 1 (15.5-ounce) can black-eyed peas, drained, rinsed
· 2 (14-ounce) cans sweet corn kernels
· 1 medium red onion, peeled, thinly sliced (about 1 cup)
· 1 large red bell pepper, seeded, deveined, chopped (about 1 cup)
· 1 large yellow bell pepper, seeded, deveined, chopped (about 1 cup)
· 1 large orange bell pepper, seeded, deveined, chopped (about 1 cup)
· 2 large jalapeño peppers, seeded, deveined, diced (about ¼ cup)
· 2 medium garlic cloves, peeled, minced (about 2 teaspoons)
· 2 tablespoons chopped fresh cilantro
· 24 mini taco shells (or substitute crisp iceberg lettuce leaves)
· Coarse salt and freshly ground pepper
· Garnishes (optional): chopped spring onions, diced avocado, light sour cream

[Z] Substitute
¼ cup + 2 tablespoons
Stevia in the Raw®
(or favorite no-calorie
sweetener).

DIRECTIONS

Place the sugar, oil and vinegar into a pot over medium heat. Bring the sauce
to a boil. Stir and cook until the sugar dissolves, about 1 minute. Cool to
room temperature.

Place the beans, black-eyed peas and corn kernels into a large bowl. Add
the onion, peppers, garlic and cilantro. Pour the sauce over the bean mixture.
Season with salt and pepper. Cover the bowl and refrigerate the beans for
8 hours or overnight.

Prepare the mini taco shells as instructed on the package. Drain the bean
mixture and place into a serving bowl. Let guests spoon beans and favorite
garnishes into the shells.

....

*Per serving 252 calories, 10 grams total fat, 1 gram saturated fat, 5 grams
monounsaturated fat, 3 grams polyunsaturated fat, 0 milligrams cholesterol,
34 grams carbohydrates, 5 grams fiber, 8 grams protein, 111 milligrams sodium*

➔ GO LEANER
*For a figure-friendly
alternative, swap
lettuce leaves for the
mini taco shells.
And have plenty of
napkins on hand!*

APRIL'S STORY
RICH LIFE ON THE CHEAP

My family is Latin, and food has always been a big part of how we connect. You can't be in one of our homes for a minute before someone asks if you'd like a bite to eat. In the low-wage neighborhood where I grew up, we ate a lot of deep-fried tacos and enchiladas and didn't have much exposure to healthier meals.

Fresh outlook. When I left home to study massage therapy, a fellow student inspired me to adopt her holistic habits. I learned new ways to prepare food and tried dishes from other cultures to expand my palate.

Healthy for less. I'm a single mom on a budget now, but I don't believe healthy eating has to cost a fortune. You can skip the fast food and expensive pre-packaged meals and sauces, and build menus around the most affordable fresh foods in your market. I use chiles, spices and lots of color to wake up dishes. (My Latin-style ratatouille with green chiles gets raves from the girls at work!)

Kid pleasers. Making meals fun and colorful also makes my 7-year-old son want to eat good-for-you food. I add dried fruit, cinnamon and crushed pecans to oatmeal, and he gobbles it up! Now I'm studying to become a pediatric nutritionist to give more kids, especially those in low-income families, the same healthy advantages.

SALADS

STARTERS, LIGHT LUNCHES & POTLUCK FARE

Wake up boring meals with these cheerful salads. Chock-full of fresh ingredients, gorgeous colors and pleasing textures, they're a treat for the eyes as well as the taste buds. For pure presentation, nothing beats the vibrant hues of the Avocado Salad with Apple Cider Vinegar *(page 38)* or the Sweet Potato Salad *(page 40)*—ideal for alfresco lunches with friends. If you're heading to a picnic or potluck, take along easy-to-pack dishes, such as the Beans, Greens & Pasta Salad *(page 32)*.

While most of the salads here work well as starters or sides, some—including the Thai Beef Salad *(page 35)* and the Colors of Health Tuna Salad *(page 36)*—can be satisfying meals by themselves. Best of all, they're loaded with antioxidants and other nutrients!

★★★ **ZUMBA ALL-STARS**
★★☆ **OCCASIONAL EATS**
★☆☆ **SOMETIME SPLURGES**

BEANS, GREENS & PASTA SALAD

FROM JANE DELL OF BAY OF PLENTY, NEW ZEALAND

THIS ONE'S A PEOPLE PLEASER AT BARBECUES!
MAKES 12 SERVINGS | TOTAL PREP/COOK TIME: 25 MINUTES ▼
★★★

INGREDIENTS
· ½ pound fresh green beans, trimmed, cut into 1-inch pieces (about 2 cups)
· 1 pound dried whole-wheat penne pasta (or substitute your favorite)
· 4 large eggs, hard-boiled, peeled, chopped
· 1 (15-ounce) can lima beans, drained, rinsed
· 1 (15-ounce) can chickpeas, drained, rinsed
· 1 medium red onion, peeled, diced (about 1 cup)
· 1 large bell pepper, seeded, deveined, diced (about 1 cup)
· 1 (10-ounce package) frozen peas, cooked, drained
· 4 ounces mixed salad greens, torn (about 4-6 cups)
· 3 tablespoons plain low-fat yogurt
· 1 tablespoon chili sauce

DIRECTIONS
To blanch green beans, plunge them into a pot of boiling, salted water and boil for 3 to 5 minutes, until they turn bright green. Use tongs or a wire strainer to transfer the beans to a large bowl of ice water and keep them immersed for 3 to 5 minutes. Drain and dry the beans.

Cook the pasta in a large pot of salted, boiling water. Drain and place the pasta into a large bowl. Add the green beans, chopped eggs, lima beans, chickpeas, onion, pepper, cooked peas and salad greens to the pasta.

In a small bowl, whisk together the yogurt and chili sauce. Pour the dressing over the salad and toss to coat. Serve immediately or cover and chill in the refrigerator.

. . . .

Per serving 236 calories, 3 grams total fat, 1 gram saturated fat, 1 gram mono-unsaturated fat, 1 gram polyunsaturated fat, 71 milligrams cholesterol, 44 grams total carbohydrates, 8 grams fiber, 13 grams protein, 179 milligrams sodium

➜ MIX IT UP!
Try different proteins, such as tuna or lean sausage. Or swap the chili sauce for a different flavor.

RAINBOW LENTIL SALAD

FROM JULIE GAUTHIER OF QUÉBEC, CANADA

MAKE THIS COLD SALAD AHEAD AND STORE IT IN THE FRIDGE.
MAKES 8 SERVINGS | TOTAL PREP/COOK TIME: 30-60 MINUTES INCLUDING TIME TO COOL ▼
★★☆

INGREDIENTS
· 1 (14-ounce) package dried lentils (about 1¾ cups)
· 1 large red bell pepper, seeded, deveined, chopped (about 1 cup)
· 1 large yellow bell pepper, seeded, deveined, chopped (about 1 cup)
· 1 large orange bell pepper, seeded, deveined, chopped (about 1 cup)
· 1 large cucumber, peeled, seeded, diced into ½-inch pieces (about 2 cups)
· 3 medium ripe tomatoes, diced (about 3 cups)
· 1 (14-ounce) can pitted, sliced black olives, drained
· 4 ounces feta cheese, diced (about 1 cup)
· 5 tablespoons white wine vinegar
· ½ teaspoon Dijon mustard
· 2 tablespoons olive oil
· Coarse salt and freshly ground pepper

DIRECTIONS
Cook the lentils according to the package directions, typically 20 to 45 minutes. Drain and cool to room temperature. Place all of the vegetables into a large bowl. Add the cooked lentils, olives and feta cheese. Whisk together the vinegar and mustard in a small bowl. Whisk in the olive oil. Pour the vinaigrette over the vegetables and toss to combine. Season with salt and pepper.

. . . .

Per serving 326 calories, 12 grams total fat, 3 grams saturated fat, 7 grams mono-unsaturated fat, 1 gram polyunsaturated fat, 13 milligrams cholesterol, 41 grams carbohydrates, 18 grams fiber, 18 grams protein, 607 milligrams sodium

SWEET BEAN SALAD

FROM ALITA HOWARD OF NEW YORK, USA

VEGANS AND MEAT EATERS ALIKE WILL LOVE THIS TANGY SALAD—A COLORFUL COMPLEMENT TO GRILLED DISHES AND OTHER SIDES AT POTLUCKS.

MAKES 12 SERVINGS | TOTAL PREP/COOK TIME: 20 MINUTES PLUS 1 HOUR TO MARINATE

★★☆

INGREDIENTS
· ½ cup olive oil
· ½ cup apple cider vinegar
· ½ cup natural granulated sugar
· 1 (15.5-ounce) can black-eyed peas, drained, rinsed
· 1 (15.5-ounce) can black beans, drained, rinsed
· 1 (14.5-ounce) can white corn, drained, rinsed
· 1 large green bell pepper, seeded, deveined, diced (about 1 cup)
· 1 large red bell pepper, seeded, deveined, diced (about 1 cup)
· 1 large red onion, peeled, diced (about 1 cup)
· 1 medium celery rib, chopped (about ⅓ cup)
· Coarse salt and freshly ground pepper

[Z] Substitute ¼ cup + 2 tablespoons Stevia in the Raw® (or favorite no-calorie sweetener).

DIRECTIONS
Whisk together the oil, vinegar and sugar in a medium saucepan over medium heat until the sugar is dissolved, about 5 to 8 minutes. Cool to room temperature.

Place the beans and corn into a large bowl. Add the vegetables. Pour the dressing over the salad and toss. The colors should look like confetti. Season with salt and pepper.

Cover and set aside for 1 hour to allow the flavors to marry. Refrigerate until ready to serve.

....

Per serving 302 calories, 10 grams total fat, 1 gram saturated fat, 7 grams monounsaturated fat, 1 gram polyunsaturated fat, 0 milligrams cholesterol, 44 grams carbohydrates, 7 grams fiber, 12 grams protein, 194 milligrams sodium

➜ **FReSH IDea**
Replace the canned beans with fresh green beans and frozen (thawed) green peas, adding a jar of chopped pimentos.

➜ **GO LeaNeR**
This recipe makes plenty of dressing. To reduce calories and fat, try cutting up to half the amount of oil, vinegar and sweetener.

→ **GOOD FAT**
Although this dish has 18 grams of total fat, 9 grams are the belly-slimming, monounsaturated variety.

GREEK BARLEY SALAD

FROM BATRICE ADAMS OF NEW JERSEY, USA

IF YOU'RE A BARLEY FAN, THE TASTE, TEXTURE AND HEALTH BENEFITS OF THIS DISH WILL MAKE IT A FAVE.

MAKES 6 SERVINGS | TOTAL PREP/COOK TIME: 50 MINUTES **V**

★★★

INGREDIENTS

· 1 cup barley
· ⅓ cup Kalamata olives, chopped
· ⅓ cup roasted red peppers, chopped
· 2 ounces feta cheese, crumbled (about ⅓ cup)
· ¼ red onion, peeled, diced (about ¼ cup)
· ¼ cup golden raisins
· 1 tablespoon chopped fresh oregano
· ⅓ cup olive oil
· 2 tablespoons red wine vinegar
· Coarse salt and freshly ground pepper

DIRECTIONS

Bring 2½ cups water to a boil in a large pot over medium-high heat. Add the barley. Reduce the heat, cover the pan with a lid and cook until all of the liquid is absorbed, about 40 minutes. Remove the pan from the heat and cool to room temperature. Once the barley is cooled, transfer to a large bowl. Add the remaining ingredients and toss to combine. Season with salt and pepper. Serve chilled or at room temperature.

· ·

Per serving 302 calories, 18 grams total fat, 3 grams saturated fat, 9 grams monounsaturated fat, 1 gram polyunsaturated fat, 8 milligrams cholesterol, 31 grams carbohydrates, 5 grams fiber, 6 grams protein, 320 milligrams sodium

THAI BEEF SALAD

FROM ANGEL MONTIER OF AUCKLAND, NEW ZEALAND

LOOKING TO BROADEN YOUR CULINARY HORIZONS? YOU'LL BE WOWED BY THE FLAVORS IN THIS SUCCULENT, ONE-DISH MEAL!

MAKES 4 SERVINGS | TOTAL PREP/COOK TIME: 30 MINUTES

★★☆

INGREDIENTS

- 1 (12- to 14-ounce) sirloin steak (or substitute flank steak)
- Coarse salt and freshly ground pepper
- 4 ounces mixed salad greens, torn (about 4-6 cups)
- 1 large red onion, peeled, diced (about 1 cup)
- ½ large cucumber, peeled, seeded, diced (about ½ cup)
- 1 medium carrot, peeled, trimmed, sliced (about ½ cup)
- 1 pint grape tomatoes, halved
- 2-3 green onions, thinly sliced (about ¼ cup)
- 2 tablespoons chopped fresh cilantro
- 1 tablespoon chopped fresh mint
- 2 tablespoons honey
- 2 tablespoons fish sauce
- 1 tablespoon low-sodium soy sauce
- 1 seranno pepper, seeded, deveined, diced (about 1 tablespoon)
- ½-inch piece fresh ginger, peeled, grated (about 1-2 teaspoons)
- 1 medium lemon, juiced (about 3 tablespoons)
- 1 large lime, juiced (about 2 tablespoons)
- 2 tablespoons sesame oil

→ **make it your own**

Add other chopped veggies to the salad. Julienned parsnip and thinly sliced fennel are fabulous options!

DIRECTIONS

Season the steak with salt and pepper. Heat a grill pan coated with vegetable oil spray over medium-high heat. Cook, turning once, until a thermometer inserted into the center of the steak reads 140°. Remove the steak to a platter and allow to rest for 10 minutes. The steak will continue to cook to medium rare. (You can cook it longer if you prefer your steak well done.)

→ **GO LIGHTER**

Many Thai dishes get their unique flavor from fish sauce, but if you're watching salt, you can eliminate up to two-thirds of the sodium here by cutting all or part of the fish sauce. Try a little more low-sodium soy sauce and an extra squirt of lime juice in its place.

Place the salad greens into a large bowl. Add the red onion, cucumber, carrot, tomatoes, green onions, cilantro and mint. Whisk together the honey, fish sauce and soy sauce in a small bowl. Stir in the pepper, ginger, lemon juice and lime juice. Whisk in the sesame oil. Toss the salad with the dressing. Thinly slice the steak. Lay the sliced steak on top of the salad.

Per serving 330 calories, 14.5 grams total fat, 4 grams saturated fat, 5.5 grams monounsaturated fat, 3 grams polyunsaturated fat, 47 milligrams cholesterol, 20 grams carbohydrates, 4 grams fiber, 28 grams protein, 961 milligrams sodium

VIETNAMESE CABBAGE & CARROT SALAD

FROM HUONG NGUYEN OF PERTH, WA, AUSTRALIA

THIS IS SIMPLE TO MAKE AHEAD SO IT'S READY WHEN YOU ARE.

MAKES 4 SERVINGS | TOTAL PREP TIME: 20 MINUTES **V**

★★★

→ GET THE BENEFITS

Each serving provides 14 grams of monounsaturated, heart-helping fat and 186% of the daily value for vitamin A, which helps strengthen your immune system and preserve your eyesight.

→ MAKE IT A MEAL

Add shredded chicken breast.

→ SODIUM WATCH

Replacing the low-sodium soy sauce with fish sauce adds a distinctive flavor, but it also adds about 420 milligrams of sodium per serving.

INGREDIENTS

- 2 large limes, juiced (3-4 tablespoons)
- 2 tablespoons low-sodium soy sauce (or substitute fish sauce)
- 1 medium garlic clove, peeled, minced (about 1 teaspoon)
- 1 small red chile, seeded, deveined, diced (about 1 teaspoon) (or substitute jalapeño pepper)
- 2 tablespoons olive oil
- ½-1 tablespoon honey
- ½ medium cabbage, shredded (about 2 cups)
- 2 medium carrots, peeled, trimmed, shredded (about 1 cup)
- 2 teaspoons chopped fresh cilantro
- 2 teaspoons chopped fresh mint
- 1 cup unsalted roasted peanuts, chopped
- Coarse salt and freshly ground pepper

DIRECTIONS

Whisk together the lime juice, soy sauce, garlic and chile in a bowl. Slowly whisk in the olive oil. Whisk in the honey until dissolved. Set the dressing aside.

Place the cabbage, carrots and herbs in a large bowl. Pour in the dressing and toss. Add the peanuts. Season with salt and pepper.

To make this dish ahead, combine all ingredients except the nuts and dressing. Cover and refrigerate. Just before serving, toss with the dressing and nuts.

....

Per serving 315 calories, 25 grams total fat, 3.5 grams saturated fat, 14 grams monounsaturated fat, 6.5 grams polyunsaturated fat, 0 milligrams cholesterol, 17 grams carbohydrates, 5 grams fiber, 10 grams protein, 330 milligrams sodium

COLORS OF HEALTH TUNA SALAD

FROM LISA ANASTASSIU OF SLIVEN, BULGARIA

SERVE IT OVER GREENS FOR A LEISURELY AFTERNOON LUNCH.

MAKES 2 SERVINGS | TOTAL PREP TIME: 15 MINUTES

★★☆

INGREDIENTS

- 1 (5-ounce) can tuna, packed in water, drained
- 1 medium ripe tomato, diced (about 1 cup)
- ½ large green or red bell pepper, seeded, deveined, chopped (about ½ cup)
- ½ large yellow bell pepper, seeded, deveined, chopped (about ½ cup)
- 2 green onions, thinly sliced (about 3 tablespoons)
- ½ cup canned kidney beans, drained, rinsed
- ½ cup canned corn, drained, rinsed
- 2 tablespoons olive oil
- 1 tablespoon red wine vinegar
- Salt and freshly ground pepper

DIRECTIONS

Place the tuna in a large bowl. Toss with the tomato, peppers, green onions, beans and corn. Whisk together the olive oil and vinegar. Pour over the salad and toss. Season with salt and pepper.

....

Per serving 320 calories, 16 grams total fat, 2 grams saturated fat, 10 grams monounsaturated fat, 2 grams polyunsaturated fat, 30 milligrams cholesterol, 27 grams carbohydrates, 6 grams fiber, 22 grams protein, 650 milligrams sodium

→ VEGETARIAN?

Skip the tuna and add any combo of nuts, seeds and homemade croutons. Try chopped walnuts—a source of protein and omega-3s.

RED & GREEN FETA SALAD

FROM LISBETH OHLSEN OF JUTLAND, DENMARK

THIS RECIPE IS ELEGANT IN ITS SIMPLICITY. FOR THE BEST FLAVOR, BUY FRESH FETA IN BLOCKS RATHER THAN IN PREPACKAGED DRY CRUMBLES.

MAKES 10 SERVINGS | TOTAL PREP/COOK TIME: 30 MINUTES **V**

★★★

INGREDIENTS
· 1 pound whole-wheat pasta (or substitute whole-grain pasta)
· 2 pints cherry tomatoes, halved
· 1 large cucumber, peeled, seeded, diced into ½-inch pieces (about 2 cups)
· 2 medium ripe avocados, seed removed, peeled, diced (about 2 cups)
· 3 medium bell peppers, seeded, deveined, chopped (about 1½ cups)
· 8 ounces feta cheese, cut into chunks (about 2 cups)
· ¼ cup olive oil
· ¼ cup white vinegar
· Freshly ground pepper

DIRECTIONS
Cook the pasta in salted boiling water according to the directions on the package. Drain and rinse under cold water. Place the pasta into a large bowl. Add all of the vegetables. Toss in the cheese.

Whisk together the oil and vinegar in a small bowl. Drizzle the dressing over the salad and season with pepper.

....

Per serving 335 calories, 16 grams total fat, 5 grams saturated fat, 8 grams monounsaturated fat, 2 grams polyunsaturated fat, 20 milligrams cholesterol, 42 grams carbohydrates, 6 grams fiber, 11 grams protein, 266 milligrams sodium

➜ **GO LEANER**
Cut the feta in half to save 40 calories and 3 grams of fat per serving. Crumble the cheese before tossing it into the salad.

➜ **WINE & DINE**
Swap the white vinegar for white wine vinegar to impart a bit of the wine's flavor to the dish.

"I pair this salad with steamed white fish for a light, Mediterranean-style meal." —LISBETH

→ **CLEAN CUTS**

Using a sharp knife, cut the avocado lengthwise around the seed. Pull the halves apart. With a firm tap, carefully wedge the knife's sharp edge into the seed. Lift and discard the seed. Cut and scoop out the meat of the avocado as shown.

AVOCADO SALAD WITH APPLE CIDER VINEGAR

FROM LISSETTE VARGAS-RODRIGUEZ OF FLORIDA, USA
★★★

THIS PAIRS WELL WITH BAKED CHICKEN OR FISH. FOR A LIGHTER SALAD, REPLACE THE AVOCADO WITH A CUCUMBER.
MAKES 2 SERVINGS | TOTAL PREP TIME: 15 MINUTES **V**

INGREDIENTS
· 1 medium ripe avocado, seed removed, peeled, diced (about 1 cup)
· 1 medium red onion, peeled, finely diced (about 1 cup)
· 1 medium ripe tomato, diced (about 1 cup)
· 1 small bunch fresh cilantro leaves, chopped (about ½ cup)
· ¼ cup apple cider vinegar
· ½ teaspoon coarse salt (or substitute garlic powder for a lower-sodium option)

DIRECTIONS
Toss the avocado, onion and tomato together in a small bowl and add the cilantro. Pour in the vinegar and mix gently to coat. Season with coarse salt.

....

Per serving 210 calories, 16 grams total fat, 2 grams saturated fat, 10 grams monounsaturated fat, 2 grams polyunsaturated fat, 0 milligrams cholesterol, 19 grams carbohydrates, 5 grams fiber, 3 grams protein, 553 milligrams sodium

LISSETTE'S STORY
STARTING OVER

At 36, I was a newly divorced mom—stressed, overweight and on statins to control my high cholesterol. Now I'm a Zumba addict, looking and feeling better than I did in high school! Here are a few tips that helped me go from a size 26 to a size 10 in about eight months:

➤ *Boot the bottled fruit juice.* There can be 300 calories in a glass! Now, if I want juice, I eat the fruit and drink lots of water.

➤ *Lunch larger.* I now eat my biggest meal in the middle of the day and eat lighter at night.

➤ *Take 20.* I heard it takes about 20 minutes to register that you're full. To avoid overeating, I serve myself half a plate of food and wait 20 minutes after eating to see if I really want more.

➤ *Include the family.* It's important that my kids stay fit, too—and exercising together is fun. I also expect them to try at least a few bites of whatever I serve at mealtime so they become adventurous eaters!

➤ *Don't obsess.* Now that I've maintained my weight loss for almost four years, I pay less attention to calories on weekends.

➤ *Celebrate!* My cholesterol has gone down so much that I'm off the statins!

39

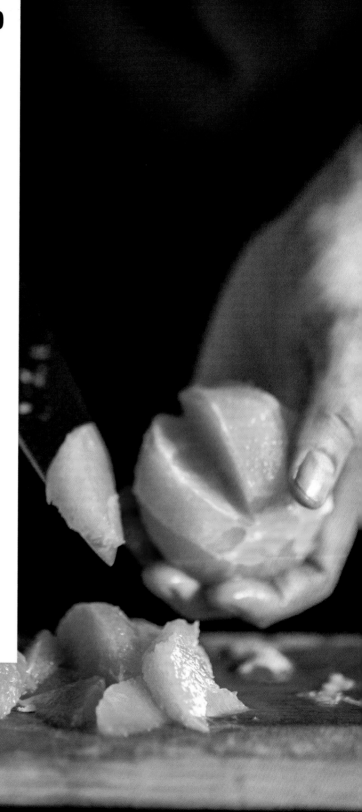

SWEET POTATO SALAD
FROM DEBORAH MANDZUK OF ALBERTA, CANADA

***IF YOU LOVE SWEET POTATOES, THIS COMBO WITH
FRESH FRUIT AND NUTS IS SURE TO BE ON YOUR HIT LIST!***
MAKES 6 SERVINGS | TOTAL PREP/COOK TIME: 45 MINUTES **V**
★★★

INGREDIENTS
· 1 large sweet potato*, diced (about 2 cups)
· 2 large apples, cored, diced (about 2 cups)
· 3 large oranges, peeled, sectioned (about 1 cup)
· 12 fresh dates, chopped (about 1 cup)
· ¾ cup unsweetened shredded coconut (reserve 1 tablespoon
  for garnish)
· ¼ cup almonds, chopped
· 1 teaspoon ground cinnamon
· 2 large limes, juiced (about ¼ cup)
· 2 tablespoons chia seeds (reserve 1 tablespoon for garnish)
· 2 teaspoons honey (optional)
· 1-inch piece fresh ginger, peeled, grated (about 1 tablespoon)

DIRECTIONS
Heat the oven to 350°. Place the diced sweet potato onto a baking
dish that has been coated with vegetable oil spray. Roast, turning
once until the potato is soft and golden. Remove from the oven and
cool to room temperature.

Place the sweet potato, apples, oranges, dates, coconut, almonds and
cinnamon in a large bowl. Whisk together the lime juice, 1 tablespoon
of the chia seeds, the honey, if using, and ginger. Drizzle the dressing
over the salad. Toss to combine. Sprinkle the remaining coconut and
chia seeds on top of the salad.

....

*Per serving 337 calories, 12 grams total fat, 7 grams saturated fat,
3.5 grams monounsaturated fat, 1 gram polyunsaturated fat, 0 milligrams
cholesterol, 52 grams carbohydrates, 11 grams fiber, 5 grams protein,
31 milligrams sodium*

*This nutrient-rich dish was submitted using a raw yam. While many foods are
safe to eat in their uncooked state, there is debate about whether yams and
sweet potatoes are among those foods. Here, we've swapped the yam for a
cooked and cooled sweet potato, but don't miss out on the benefits of eating
raw. *Read Deborah's story on page 18.*

➜ **CHIA MI AMORE**
A great source of omega-3s, chia seeds can be found online or at natural-foods markets.

COOKING CHICKEN

To make sure that you have flavorful, moist chicken for any salad, roast chicken breasts on the bone. Preheat the oven to 450°. Place the chicken breasts on a baking sheet, season with salt and pepper, drizzle with olive oil and place in the oven. Reduce heat to 350° and roast the chicken 25 to 30 minutes. It is cooked when its juices run clear and the meat can be pierced with a knife. Cool to room temperature. Remove the skin and bones, and cut the chicken as called for in the recipe.

→ SMOKIN'!
Liquid smoke is a seasoning that mimics the flavor of food cooked using wood chips, such as hickory and mesquite. Find it in the condiment aisle in your grocery.

CHICKEN & SPINACH SALAD WITH SMOKY DRESSING

FROM SARAH WINTERS OF OHIO, USA

THE RECIPE MAKES MORE DRESSING THAN YOU MAY NEED. STORE THE EXTRA IN THE FRIDGE AND TRY IT WITH COOKED TURKEY.
MAKES 4 SERVINGS | TOTAL PREP/COOK TIME: 15 MINUTES PLUS TIME TO COOK CHICKEN
★★☆

INGREDIENTS
· 2 cups cooked chicken (*see facing page*), diced or shredded
· ½ pound fresh spinach leaves, chopped (about 2 cups)
· ½ small red onion, peeled, finely diced (about ¼ cup)
· 1 medium Granny Smith apple, peeled, cored, diced (about 1 cup)
· ¼ cup plain low-fat yogurt
· ¼ cup apple cider vinegar
· 1 tablespoon whole-grain mustard
· 1 tablespoon honey
· ½ teaspoon liquid smoke flavoring
· Coarse salt and freshly ground pepper
· 2 tablespoons sunflower seeds

DIRECTIONS
Place the cooked chicken into a bowl with the spinach leaves, onion and apple. For the dressing, whisk together the yogurt, vinegar, mustard, honey and liquid smoke. Drizzle enough of the dressing to just moisten the salad. Toss and season with salt and pepper. Sprinkle the sunflower seeds over the top.

....

Per serving 238 calories, 6 grams total fat, 1 gram saturated fat, 1.5 grams monounsaturated fat, 2 grams polyunsaturated fat, 72 milligrams cholesterol, 16 grams carbohydrates, 3.5 grams fiber, 30 grams protein, 138 milligrams sodium

NEW COMFORT FOODS

Many of the recipes here—including the Vegetarian Posole *(page 49)*, Middle Eastern Sleek *(page 57)* and Moro de Habichuelas Rojas *(page 58)*—are fresh takes on traditional favorites from different regions of the world. They're feel-good foods—rich, aromatic dishes that instantly boost your mood.

And they're so versatile! You can customize soups with different bases, veggies or seasonings. Try turkey sausage instead of ham in the International Black Bean & Ham Soup *(page 48)* or vegetable broth instead of chicken in the Butternut Squash Soup *(page 51)*. Get creative!

....

★★★ ZUMBA ALL-STARS
★★☆ OCCASIONAL EATS
★☆☆ SOMETIME SPLURGES

SOUPS & SIDES

INTERNATIONAL BLACK BEAN & HAM SOUP

FROM SANDRA JENNINGS OF CONNECTICUT, USA

OH, THAT HEADY AROMA! YOU WON'T WANT TO LEAVE THE KITCHEN.
MAKES 8 SERVINGS | TOTAL PREP/COOK TIME: 1 HOUR, 35 MINUTES PLUS TIME TO SOAK BEANS OVERNIGHT 🌶
★★☆

INGREDIENTS
· 1 pound dried black beans (about 2 cups)
· 1 pound cooked ham, diced into cubes (or substitute lower-sodium cooked ham)
· 1 (28-ounce) can diced tomatoes
· 1 medium onion, peeled, diced (about 1 cup)
· 1 (7-ounce) can chopped, marinated green chiles
· 3 large garlic cloves, peeled, minced (about 1 tablespoon)
· 2 teaspoons ground cumin
· 1 teaspoon paprika
· 1 teaspoon ground coriander seed
· 1 teaspoon ground cardamom
· 1 teaspoon ground chipotle pepper
· Coarse salt
· Plain 2% Greek yogurt or light sour cream for garnish (optional)

DIRECTIONS
Soak the dry beans in 6 cups cold water overnight. Drain and rinse.

Place the beans in a large pot with 6 cups of water over medium-high heat. Cover and bring to a boil. Reduce the heat to medium low and cook until the beans are tender, about 45 minutes. Add the ham and pour in the tomatoes. Stir in the onion, chiles and garlic. Stir in the ground spices—cumin, paprika, coriander seed, cardamom and chipotle pepper. Season with salt. Cook over medium heat until the beans and veggies are soft, about 45 minutes. Ladle into bowls and serve with a dollop of yogurt or light sour cream if desired.

. . . .

Per serving 310 calories, 7 grams total fat, 2 grams saturated fat, 3 grams monounsaturated fat, 1 gram polyunsaturated fat, 32 milligrams cholesterol, 41 grams carbohydrates, 9 grams fiber, 22 grams protein, 762 milligrams sodium

➜ **CHOICES, CHOICES!**
For a variation, replace ham with sliced chicken or turkey sausage, or omit the ham and make it vegetarian!

SPICY LENTIL SOUP

FROM JULIE KARKAR OF OXFORDSHIRE, ENGLAND

THIS NUTRITIOUS AND DELICIOUS DISH MAKES A FILLING LUNCH.
MAKES 8 SERVINGS | TOTAL PREP/COOK TIME: 1 HOUR, 10 MINUTES **V** 🌶
★★★

INGREDIENTS
· 1 tablespoon olive oil
· 1 large white onion, peeled, diced (about 1½ cups)
· 3 medium carrots, peeled, trimmed, diced (about 1½ cups)
· 1 large russet potato, peeled, diced (about 1½ cups)
· 3 medium celery ribs, sliced (about 1 cup)
· 3 medium garlic cloves, peeled, minced (about 1 tablespoon)
· 1 tablespoon ground cumin
· 2 teaspoons paprika
· 1 teaspoon chili powder
· 1 teaspoon ground ginger
· 1 (28-ounce) can diced tomatoes
· 2 tablespoons tomato purée
· 1 quart homemade or prepared low-sodium vegetable broth
· 1 (14-ounce) package dried lentils (about 1¾ cups)
· Coarse salt and freshly ground pepper

DIRECTIONS
Heat the oil in a large soup pot over medium-high heat. Place the onion, carrots, potato, celery and garlic into the pan. Cook until soft, about 10 minutes. Stir in the cumin, paprika, chili powder and ginger. Cook for 1 minute more. Pour in the tomatoes, tomato purée and vegetable broth. Rinse the lentils and add to the pot. Bring the soup to a boil. Reduce the heat to low and cook until the vegetables are soft and the lentils are cooked through, about 45 minutes.

. . . .

Per serving 256 calories, 2.5 grams total fat, 0 grams saturated fat, 1.5 grams monounsaturated fat, 0 grams polyunsaturated fat, 0 milligrams cholesterol, 45 grams carbohydrates, 18 grams fiber, 15 grams protein, 222 milligrams sodium

VEGETARIAN POSOLE

FROM ALEXANDRA TRAN OF CALIFORNIA, USA

SPICE UP YOUR DAY WITH THIS NO-MEAT VERSION OF THE TRADITIONAL MEXICAN SOUP.

MAKES 4 SERVINGS | TOTAL PREP/COOK TIME: 1 HOUR **V** 🌶

★★☆

INGREDIENTS

· 1 small-medium onion, peeled, diced, divided
 (about ½ cup + 2 tablespoons for ancho chile liquid)
· 3 garlic cloves, peeled, chopped, divided
· 1 jalapeño, diced (about 2 tablespoons)
· 3 teaspoons olive oil, divided
· 1 tablespoon chili powder (or add more for a spicier soup)
· 5 cups homemade or prepared low-sodium vegetable broth
 (plus more if needed)
· Coarse salt and freshly ground pepper
· 1 cup firm tofu, cubed
· 2 cups hominy, drained, rinsed
· 2 ancho chile peppers
· Garnishes (optional): sliced avocado, lime wedges, shredded green cabbage,
 sliced radishes, chopped cilantro, diced onion, baked tostada shell pieces

→ **AUTHENTICITY**

To achieve the red color in traditional posole, you can add some enchilada sauce.

DIRECTIONS

In a medium-sized pot over medium heat, sauté ½ cup of the diced onion, 2 cloves of chopped garlic and the jalapeño in 2 teaspoons of olive oil until the onion is translucent, about 7 to 8 minutes. Stir in the chili powder and cook a few minutes more. Pour in the vegetable broth and season with salt and pepper. Bring to a boil. Cover and reduce heat. Simmer for 10 minutes.

While simmering the broth, heat 1 teaspoon of olive oil in a skillet and sauté the tofu over medium-high heat for 2 to 3 minutes, turning to cook all sides. Add the tofu to the broth. Stir in the hominy. Cover and simmer for 15 minutes or longer to allow flavors to meld. Add more vegetable broth as needed.

While soup is simmering, boil the ancho chiles in a small pot of water until soft, about 15 minutes. Place chiles in a blender with 1½ cups of water and the remaining diced onion and garlic. Add salt and pepper. Blend and strain the mixture in a sieve to separate the liquid from the pulp. Place the strained liquid in a small bowl to serve with other garnishes. Discard the pulp, or if you like a *really* spicy soup, add it to the soup pot.

Invite guests to spoon some of the ancho chile liquid into individual soup bowls for spice and top with favorite garnishes.

....

Per serving 175 calories, 7 grams total fat, 1 gram saturated fat, 3 grams monoun-saturated fat, 2.5 grams polyunsaturated fat, 0 milligrams cholesterol, 24 grams carbohydrates, 5 grams fiber, 9 grams protein, 489 milligrams sodium

"I love posole—one of the first Mexican dishes I learned to make! The original can be very fattening, so I created a leaner version to suit my healthy lifestyle." —ALEXANDRA

➜ **make more**
Soups are a great time-saver. Double the recipe, freeze extra portions and thaw when you need something quick and easy.

Small rustic blue bowls, ABC Homes

BUTTERNUT SQUASH SOUP

MELISSA LOPEZ OF NEW YORK, USA

IT'S THE PERFECT COMFORT FOOD FOR A CHILLY EVENING.

MAKES 4 SERVINGS | TOTAL PREP/COOK TIME: 50 MINUTES

★★☆

INGREDIENTS

· 2 tablespoons unsalted butter
· 1 whole leek, washed, white parts chopped (about 1 cup)
· 2 cups homemade or prepared low-sodium chicken broth
· ½ medium white onion, peeled, chopped (about ½ cup)
· ⅛ teaspoon ground cumin
· ½ medium butternut squash, peeled, diced into ¼-inch squares (about 2 cups)
· 1 medium carrot, peeled, trimmed, chopped (about ½ cup)
· ½ teaspoon ground cinnamon
· ½ teaspoon ground ginger
· ½ cup half-and-half
· Coarse salt and freshly ground pepper
· Toasted pumpkin seeds or pine nuts for garnish (optional)

[Z] Substitute 2 tablespoons canola oil.

DIRECTIONS

Heat the butter in a large pot over medium-high heat. Add the leek, onion and cumin. Cook until the leek is soft, about 5 minutes. Pour in the chicken broth. Add the squash and carrot. Season with cinnamon and ginger. Bring the soup to a boil. Reduce the heat to medium low and cook until all of the vegetables are soft, about 15 minutes.

Emulsify the soup using a food processor or handheld immersion blender. Pour in the half-and-half. Season with salt and pepper.

....

Per serving 171 calories, 10 grams total fat, 6 grams saturated fat, 3 grams monounsaturated fat, 1 gram polyunsaturated fat, 27 milligrams cholesterol, 17 grams carbohydrates, 3 grams fiber, 5 grams protein, 148 milligrams sodium

➜ MAKE IT VEGETARIAN

Replace chicken broth with homemade or prepared low-sodium vegetable broth.

LEBANESE CUCUMBER SOUP

FROM SANDIE WILLIAMS OF WORCESTERSHIRE, ENGLAND

THIS REFRESHING SOUP REQUIRES NO COOKING! YOU CAN ALSO TRY VEGETABLE BROTH IN PLACE OF THE MILK.
MAKES 8 SERVINGS | TOTAL PREP TIME: 15 MINUTES PLUS 30 MINUTES TO REFRIGERATE **V**
★★☆

INGREDIENTS
· 2 large cucumbers, peeled, chopped (about 3 cups)
· 2 small garlic cloves, peeled, minced, mashed to a paste
· pinch of salt (about ⅛ teaspoon)
· 2 pints plain 2% Greek yogurt
· ½ small lemon, juiced (about 2 teaspoons)
· 1 teaspoon natural granulated sugar
· ½ cup whole milk
· 3 tablespoons chopped fresh mint, divided
· Freshly ground black pepper
· Diced cucumber for garnish (optional)

[Z] Substitute 1 teaspoon Stevia in the Raw® (or favorite no-calorie sweetener).

DIRECTIONS
Place the cucumbers into the bowl of a food processor. Mix salt into the garlic paste and add it to the bowl along with the yogurt, lemon juice and sugar. Pulse until smooth. Pour in the milk and mix. Transfer the soup to a chilled tureen or large serving bowl. Stir in 2 tablespoons of the mint. Cover the bowl and refrigerate for at least 30 minutes.

Ladle the soup into individual bowls. Garnish with pepper, the remaining mint and diced cucumber.

....

Per serving 110 calories, 3 grams total fat, 2 grams saturated fat, 0 grams monounsaturated fat, 0 grams polyunsaturated fat, 10 milligrams cholesterol, 8 grams carbohydrates, 0 grams fiber, 12 grams protein, 81 milligrams sodium

→ **NO FOOD PROCESSOR?**
*Grate cucumbers,
place in a sieve,
sprinkle lightly with
salt and let drain for
30 minutes before
adding to the other
ingredients.*

TRICKED-OUT TORTILLA SOUP

FROM JESSIE VILLARREAL OF WASHINGTON, USA

THIS ONE'S A HEARTY MEAL ALL BY ITSELF!

MAKES 8 SERVINGS | TOTAL PREP/COOK TIME: 30 MINUTES PLUS 6-8 HOURS UNATTENDED IN SLOW COOKER

★★☆

INGREDIENTS

· 1 whole (4- to 5-pound) cooked rotisserie chicken (available in many supermarkets), skin and bones removed, shredded (*or cook your own—see "Cooking Chicken," page 44*)
· 1 large white onion, peeled, diced (about 1½ cups)
· 1 (10-ounce) package frozen corn, thawed
· 1 (28-ounce) can diced tomatoes
· 1 (14-ounce) can red enchilada sauce (or substitute lower-sodium homemade enchilada sauce)
· 1 (14-ounce) can black beans, drained
· 1 large jalapeño pepper, seeded, veins removed, diced (about 2 tablespoons) (or substitute 1 serrano pepper for a hotter dish)
· 2 tablespoons chopped fresh cilantro
· 2 medium garlic cloves, peeled, minced (about 2 teaspoons)
· 2½ cups homemade or prepared low-sodium chicken broth
· 1 teaspoon cumin
· 1 teaspoon chili powder
· Freshly ground pepper
· Garnishes (optional): home-baked tortilla strips (*see facing page*), chopped onion, diced avocado, light sour cream, a squeeze of lime

DIRECTIONS

Place all of the ingredients into a slow cooker. Cook on the low setting for 6 to 8 hours. Add garnishes as desired.

....

Per serving 410 calories, 13 grams total fat, 3 grams saturated fat, 4 grams monounsaturated fat, 3 grams polyunsaturated fat, 120 milligrams cholesterol, 28 grams carbohydrates, 6 grams fiber, 46 grams protein, 770 milligrams sodium

➜ **IF YOU'VE GOT THE TIME**

A store-bought rotisserie chicken and canned enchilada sauce make quick work of this easy, throw-together dish. For a more authentic soup—or to control the amount of sodium—you can make your own sauce. Search keywords "low sodium enchilada sauce" online to discover a variety of low-salt recipes.

SERVE IT UP

Home-baked tortilla strips are a healthy alternative to store-bought chips. To make them, buy corn tortillas, spray both sides of each tortilla with vegetable oil spray and cut the tortillas into thin strips using a pizza wheel. Place the strips on a cookie sheet and bake in a preheated oven at 400° for about 12 minutes or until crisp at the edges.

To serve, add a few strips to each bowl of soup along with other favorite garnishes.

zlife *presents*

►► VEGETABLE SOUP

FROM BETTY McGUINNESS OF FLORIDA, USA
PUBLISHER, *Z-LIFE* MAGAZINE

YOU CAN ADD OTHER FAVORITE VEGGIES AND LEGUMES
TO GIVE THIS SIMPLE SOUP YOUR PERSONAL TOUCH.
MAKES 6 SERVINGS | TOTAL PREP/COOK TIME: 50 MINUTES
★★★

→ MAKE IT A MEAL

Add canned chickpeas, black-eyed peas or kidney beans and a piece of multi-grain bread.

INGREDIENTS
· 4 teaspoons olive oil
· 2 medium yellow onions, diced (about 2 cups)
· 2 celery stalks, diced (about 1 cup)
· 2 small carrots, diced (about 1 cup)
· Salt and freshly ground pepper
· 1 cup corn kernels, fresh cut from the cob or frozen (thawed)
· 3 parsnips, diced (about 2 cups)
· ¾ pound Brussels sprouts, quartered (about 3 cups)
· 1 (32-ounce) container prepared low-sodium chicken stock
· 5 tablespoons unsalted tomato paste
· 4 tablespoons chopped fresh parsley
· 1 tablespoon fresh lemon juice

DIRECTIONS

Heat the olive oil in a stock pot over medium-high heat. Add the onions, celery and carrots and season with salt and pepper. Sweat the vegetables until the onion is translucent, about 5 minutes. Add the corn kernels, parsnip and Brussels sprouts and continue to cook, stirring occasionally, until the vegetables begin to caramelize, about 15 minutes.

Add the chicken stock and tomato paste and bring to a simmer. Turn off the heat and stir in the parsley and lemon juice.

· ·

Per serving 160 calories, 3.5 grams total fat, .5 gram saturated fat, 2.5 grams monounsaturated fat, .5 gram polyunsaturated fat, 0 milligrams cholesterol, 29 grams carbohydrates, 7 grams fiber, 6 grams protein, 108 milligrams sodium

BETTY'S STORY
SHARING THE LOVE

As a reward to myself for losing 30 pounds, I fulfilled a longtime dream of going to culinary school. I wanted to be in a field that promotes joy and healthy living, so while I continued to work in magazine publishing, I completed a New York-based chef-training program that emphasizes natural, vegetarian cooking.

Instructors taught students to think of the pantry as our medicine cabinet. We learned to make tasty, healthy dishes that I still enjoy serving to family and friends.

Although I ultimately chose not to become a professional chef, I'm proud to have the skills—and I'm even prouder to be working now with one of the most exciting fitness companies in the world. The positive and contagious attitude of our Zumba family is inspiring, and through *Z-LIFE*, I get to bring fans joy and healthy living all year!

MIDDLE EASTERN SLEEK

FROM ASHLEY POUND OF PENNSYLVANIA, USA
EDITOR, *ZUMBA LOVERS COOKBOOK*

THE NAME "SLEEK" COMES FROM "SILIQ," ARABIC FOR SWISS CHARD—AN INGREDIENT TRADITIONALLY USED IN THIS FAVORITE SYRIAN SIDE DISH. HERE, KALE IS THE VEGGIE OF CHOICE.
MAKES 8 SERVINGS | TOTAL PREP/COOK TIME: 55 MINUTES **V**
★ ★ ★

INGREDIENTS
· ½ cup whole-grain bulgur wheat, uncooked
· 1 cup prepared low-sodium vegetable broth (or substitute water)
· 3 tablespoons olive oil
· 1 medium sweet onion, peeled, cut into thin 1-inch-long strips (about 1 cup)
· 2 bunches kale (about 1½ pounds), washed, center ribs removed, chopped (about 16 cups)
· 1 (15.5-ounce) can black-eyed peas, drained, rinsed
· Coarse salt and freshly ground pepper
· Lemon juice
· Garnishes (optional): lemon wedges, plain 2% Greek yogurt or plain soy yogurt

DIRECTIONS
Rinse the bulgur thoroughly in a sieve to remove dust and grit and transfer to a bowl. Heat broth (or use hot tap water) and pour over the bulgur until fully covered. Let the bulgur soak for at least 30 minutes. (You can also soak it overnight in an airtight container placed in the fridge.)

While the bulgur is soaking, add 2 tablespoons olive oil and the chopped onion to a large, deep nonstick skillet or wok. Brown the onions over medium-low heat to caramelize, about 10 minutes. Stir occasionally. Sprinkle a little water over the onions halfway through cooking to keep them from drying out.

When the onions are caramelized, add 1 tablespoon oil. Add the chopped kale. (You don't need to dry the kale after washing. Let some of the moisture go into the pan.) The skillet or wok will be very full. Season with salt and pepper and cover with a lid. Cook on low heat, about 15 minutes, until the kale is wilted and reduced in volume. Stir occasionally to mix with the oil and onions.

The bulgur should now be soft. Drain any liquid that it has not absorbed and stir the bulgur into the cooked kale. Stir in the black-eyed peas. Season with salt and pepper and sprinkle liberally with lemon juice. Mix well and cook another 10 minutes at low heat, stirring occasionally. If desired, garnish with lemon wedges and yogurt on the side.

....

Per serving 200 calories, 6 grams total fat, 1 gram saturated fat, 4 grams monounsaturated fat, 1 gram polyunsaturated fat, 0 milligrams cholesterol, 32 grams carbohydrates, 6 grams fiber, 8 grams protein, 300 milligrams sodium

SUPERSTAR KALE

Kale is one of the planet's most nutrient- and antioxidant-rich foods—known for reducing inflammation, improving bone health, fighting signs of aging and boosting the immune system! This leafy veggie is tastiest and most abundant during cool-weather months, when many other greens are out of season. But be choosy about how you buy and cook it: *Quality matters.* Kale that sits too long on a grocery shelf can lose flavor or become bitter. Buy it at natural-foods markets or farmers' markets where fresh produce is offered daily.

Kale should be dark green with no yellowing or wilting. Favor smaller, young leaves—typically sweeter and more tender than mature ones. *Get all the good stuff.* Some recipes call for the kale to be boiled before adding it to other ingredients. This one lets kale steam in the skillet or wok, retaining more of its nutrients.

MORO DE HABICHUELAS ROJAS (RED BEANS & RICE)

DAVID QUARLES OF TENNESSEE, USA

A TRADITIONAL DOMINICAN CREOLE DISH GETS A HEALTHY OVERHAUL.

MAKES 8 SERVINGS | TOTAL PREP/COOK TIME: 1 HOUR, 10 MINUTES Ⓥ 🌶

★★★

INGREDIENTS

· 2 tablespoons olive oil, divided
· 5 Roma tomatoes, diced (about 1 cup)
· 1 small yellow onion, peeled, finely diced (about ½ cup)
· 1 medium bell pepper, seeded, veins removed, chopped (about ½ cup)
· 1 medium celery rib, sliced (about ¼ cup)
· 1 large jalapeño pepper, seeded, veins removed, diced (about 2 tablespoons)
· 1 large garlic clove, peeled, minced (about 1 teaspoon)
· 1 teaspoon dried cilantro
· ½ teaspoon ground oregano
· Coarse salt and freshly ground pepper
· ¼ cup red wine
· 2 tablespoons bitter orange juice (such as Goya® brand)
· 2 tablespoons tomato paste
· 2 (15.5-ounce) cans red kidney beans, drained, rinsed
· 2 cups uncooked brown rice

DIRECTIONS

In a deep pot, heat 1 tablespoon olive oil over medium-high heat. Add the tomatoes, onion, peppers, celery and garlic. Cook until the veggies are soft, about 5 minutes. Stir in the cilantro and oregano. Season with salt and pepper. Pour in the wine and bitter orange juice and stir in the tomato paste. Add the beans and stir. Add the rice. Pour in 4 cups of water, stirring well. Bring to a boil.

Reduce the heat to medium low. Cover the pan and cook until all of the liquid has been absorbed and the rice is firm, about 35 to 40 minutes. Adjust the seasonings. Drizzle with the remaining 1 tablespoon olive oil.

....

Per serving 318 calories, 5 grams total fat, 1 gram saturated fat, 3 grams monounsaturated fat, 1 gram polyunsaturated fat, 0 milligrams cholesterol, 58 grams carbohydrates, 9 grams fiber, 10 grams protein, 272 milligrams sodium

DAVID'S STORY
IMPROVING ON TRADITION

Cooking is something my family really enjoys—and when we make meals from our Latin heritage, we enjoy it even more. Many of the Caribbean-influenced dishes we love are high in flavor but also high in salt, oil and other ingredients that aren't healthy in big doses. With diabetes and high blood pressure running in my family, I like to invent healthier ways to prepare these dishes.

A new standard. This modification to one of my favorites, red beans and rice, is a good example. After a few test runs, I was able to perfect the recipe with ingredients recommended by my nutritionist. It's now a popular dish at family gatherings and social functions.

Big changes. By changing my diet and increasing my daily activity, I've gone from 265 to 180 pounds! Zumba Fitness has been the catalyst and my main source of motivation. I could not be more appreciative of this life-changing experience.

SPICY CHICKPEAS WITH SPINACH

FROM CYNTHIA MELAND OF BLOMMENHOLM, NORWAY

SO SIMPLE TO MAKE! IT'S A PERFECT COMPLEMENT TO CURRIED CHICKEN AND OTHER INDIAN ENTRÉES.

MAKES 4 SERVINGS | TOTAL PREP/COOK TIME: 25 MINUTES **V** 🌶

★★☆

INGREDIENTS

· 1 tablespoon olive oil
· 1 medium yellow onion, peeled, finely diced (about 1 cup)
· 1 medium garlic clove, peeled, minced (about 1 teaspoon)
· 1 (14.5-ounce) can low-sodium diced tomatoes
· 1 small red chile, seeded, veins removed, diced (about 1 teaspoon)
· 2 (15.5-ounce) cans chickpeas, drained, rinsed
· 1 pound fresh spinach leaves (about 4 cups)
· Coarse salt and freshly ground pepper

DIRECTIONS

Heat the olive oil in a skillet over medium-high heat. Add the onion and garlic and cook until soft, about 5 minutes. Add the tomatoes, chile and chickpeas. Reduce the heat and cook for 10 minutes more. Add the spinach and cook until wilted. Season with salt and pepper.

....

Per serving 338 calories, 6 grams total fat, 1 gram saturated fat, 3 grams monounsaturated fat, 2 grams polyunsaturated fat, 0 milligrams cholesterol, 60 grams carbohydrates, 12 grams fiber, 13 grams protein, 480 milligrams sodium

➜ **make it a meal**

Serve with brown rice for a light, vegan dinner that's sure to please!

"My nutrition philosophy is simple: If you take care of your body, it will take care of you. Then you'll have more energy to take care of others." —CYNTHIA

zlife *presents* ®

▸▸ BROCCOLI WITH PEANUT SAUCE

FROM LISA CAIN OF MASSACHUSETTS, USA
CEO, SNACK-GIRL.COM

COOKING WITH FAMILIAR INGREDIENTS LIKE PEANUT BUTTER IS A CLEVER WAY TO GET KIDS TO EAT VEGGIES. SHARE THE FUN BY LETTING THEM HELP MEASURE AND STIR!

MAKES 6 SERVINGS | TOTAL PREP/COOK TIME: 15 MINUTES **V**

★★☆

INGREDIENTS

· 2 pounds broccoli, cleaned, trimmed, separated into stems and florets, stems chopped (about 4 cups)
· ¼ cup smooth peanut butter
· 2 tablespoons rice vinegar, seasoned (or plain)
· 2 tablespoons low-sodium soy sauce
· 1 teaspoon natural granulated sugar ⎤
· 1 garlic clove, minced (optional)
· ½ teaspoon ground ginger (optional)

[Z] Substitute 1 teaspoon Stevia in the Raw® (or favorite no-calorie sweetener).

→ **EXPERIMENT!**

Replace the peanut butter with another favorite nut or seed butter such as almond, cashew or sunflower.

DIRECTIONS

Steam the broccoli in a steamer basket over boiling water or in a large covered pot with ¼-inch boiling water for 3 to 5 minutes, until crisp-tender. In a small bowl, mix the peanut butter, rice vinegar, soy sauce and sugar, along with the garlic and ginger if using.

If you store peanut butter in the refrigerator, heat it for about 30 seconds to help it mix well with the other ingredients. Stir the mixture vigorously until combined. Pour the sauce into a small serving bowl and invite guests to spoon it over the steamed broccoli.

....

Per serving 82 calories, 5.5 grams total fat, 1 gram saturated fat, 2.5 grams monounsaturated fat, 1.5 grams polyunsaturated fat, 0 milligrams cholesterol, 6 grams carbohydrates, 1 gram fiber, 4 grams protein, 215 milligrams sodium

MAIN DISHES

ENTRÉES, STIR-FRIES & ONE-POT MEALS

Among the recipes submitted, chicken was an overwhelming favorite and appears in dishes across the cultural spectrum—from Chicken Vermont (*page 91*) to Chicken Saag Aloo Curry (*page 92*). But there's something here to satisfy every palate and preference. Vegetarians can get excited about Thai Curried Vegetables (*page 78*), Nori Veggie Rolls (*page 96*) or Channa Masala (*page 100*), while seafood fans will enjoy Whole Red Snapper with Rosemary (*page 108*) or Ceviche with Sweet Potatoes & Yuca (*page 110*). Are you a meat lover? Go for the Hometown Meatloaf (*page 76*) or Lettuce-Wrap Tacos (*page 105*). Choices, choices!

....

★★★ ZUMBA ALL-STARS
★★☆ OCCASIONAL EATS
★☆☆ SOMETIME SPLURGES

"For me, paella cooked over an open fire evokes the beauty of my second home, Valencia, Spain—the ocean, the history, the passion." —*PATRICIA*

SEAFOOD "PAELLA" WITH QUINOA

FROM PATRICIA DONERSON OF STUTTGART, GERMANY

BASED ON TRADITIONAL PAELLA VALENCIANA, THIS VERSION REPLACES PAELLA RICE WITH SUPERFOOD QUINOA.

MAKES 8 SERVINGS | TOTAL PREP/COOK TIME: 1 HOUR

★★☆

INGREDIENTS

· 1 tablespoon olive oil
· ½ pound fresh string beans, cut into 1-inch pieces
· 1 large red bell pepper, seeded, deveined, chopped (about 1 cup)
· 1 large yellow bell pepper, seeded, deveined, chopped (about 1 cup)
· 2 medium garlic cloves, peeled, minced (about 2 teaspoons)
· 1 (14.5-ounce) can diced tomatoes
· Coarse salt and freshly ground pepper
· 2 quarts homemade or prepared low-sodium chicken broth
· ½ teaspoon saffron threads
· 1 cup quinoa
· 1 pound fresh jumbo shrimp, peeled, deveined (21-25)
· 2 (6- to 8-ounce) tilapia fillets, cut into 2-inch pieces
· 1 pound mussels, scrubbed (about 20)
· ½ pint cherry tomatoes, halved
· 4 lemons, quartered

DIRECTIONS

Heat the olive oil in a large, deep skillet (with lid) over medium-high heat. Add the string beans, bell peppers and garlic to the pan. Cook until soft, about 5 minutes. Pour in the diced tomatoes. Season with salt and pepper.

Heat the broth in a saucepan over medium heat. Stir in the saffron. Cook for 3 to 5 minutes. The broth will turn a rich yellow color.

Place the quinoa in the skillet with the vegetables and stir. Add the shrimp and the tilapia. Pour in the broth gradually until the quinoa is just covered but the pan is not completely full.

Cover the pan and reduce the heat to medium low. Cook for 10 minutes. Add the mussels and cherry tomatoes to the pan and cook until all the mussels have opened, about 10 minutes more. (If any mussels do not open, discard them.)

Place the skillet on a trivet in the middle of the table and serve family-style, with lemon wedges to squeeze over the paella.

....

Per serving 333 calories, 8 grams total fat, 1 gram saturated fat, 3 grams monounsaturated fat, 2 grams polyunsaturated fat, 155 milligrams cholesterol, 29 grams carbohydrates, 4 grams fiber, 38 grams protein, 1,097 milligrams sodium

PATRICIA'S STORY
NO EXTREMES

I shed 33 pounds in five months, but it wasn't by drastically changing my eating habits. I still enjoy my food!

Knowing I wouldn't stick to a fully sketched-out meal plan, I consulted a nutritionist for some basic guidelines, found the right balance of eating and physical activity for me and started paying more attention to carbs and sweets. Over time, I learned to substitute healthier ingredients in the dishes I love and started experimenting with recipes.

Calorie burning. Now that I'm a Zumba instructor, I move my body a lot more than I used to, so it craves more energy. I eat a healthy balance of carbs, veggies and protein for six days and then reward myself with an "off" day. A little more nutritional sinning than usual is just an excuse for more Zumba dancing!

Staying motivated. I keep pictures taken of myself before losing the weight so I can say, "Wow! I look so toned now." If the scale moves in the wrong direction, I don't starve myself like I've done in the past. I just tell myself it's time to sweat! Hearing my students' excitement when we shake it to the music is the best reward ever, and compliments from friends, family and even strangers tell me I'm doing something right!

FLAVOR INFUSION

Choose a chile-infused olive oil with a high smoke point (see page 22) or substitute a chile-infused avocado oil, such as Olivado® brand, for stability at medium-high heat.

KING PRAWN CHILI PASTA

FROM CLAIRE HANSON OF NORTHUMBERLAND, UK

WAKE UP YOUR SENSES WITH THIS SPICY SEAFOOD-AND-VEGGIE MIX!

MAKES 4 SERVINGS | TOTAL PREP/COOK TIME: 30 MINUTES

★★☆

INGREDIENTS

· 8 ounces whole-wheat pasta
· 2 tablespoons chile-infused olive oil, divided
· 1 pound fresh king prawns (shrimp), peeled, deveined (10-15)
· ½ pound asparagus spears (about 16), sliced into 1-inch pieces (about 2 cups)
· 2 small red chiles, seeded, deveined, diced (about 3 tablespoons)
· Zest of 3 medium limes (about 1½ tablespoons)

DIRECTIONS

Cook the pasta in a large pot of boiling, salted water. Heat 1 tablespoon of the oil in a wok or pan over medium-high heat. Cook the prawns in the oil, turning once until just opaque, about 3 to 4 minutes. Toss in the asparagus and red chiles. Stir in the lime zest. Drain the pasta and add to the prawns, tossing well. Reduce the heat to medium and cook for 1 minute. Drizzle the remaining oil over the top.

Per serving 396 calories, 10 grams total fat, 1 gram saturated fat, 5 grams monoun-saturated fat, 2 grams polyunsaturated fat, 173 milligrams cholesterol, 47 grams carbohydrates, 6 grams fiber, 33 grams protein, 174 milligrams sodium

zlife
presents

▸▸ **CAIPIRINHA-GLAZED SHRIMP SKEWERS**

FROM CATHERINE DE ORIO OF ILLINOIS, USA
EDITOR-IN-CHIEF, CULINARYCURATOR.COM & GLAMOURGRUB.COM

INSPIRED BY A BRAZILIAN COCKTAIL—AND A FAVORITE ZUMBA SONG—THIS DISH MAKES YOU FEEL LIKE YOU'RE ON A TROPICAL ISLAND HOLIDAY!
MAKES 4 SERVINGS | TOTAL PREP/COOK TIME: 1 HOUR, 15 MINUTES
★★☆

INGREDIENTS
Shrimp & Glaze
· 1 pound fresh jumbo shrimp with tails, peeled, deveined (20-24)
· 4 sugarcane swizzle sticks, each trimmed to a point at one end to form a skewer
· Kosher salt and freshly ground pepper
· ½ cup cachaça
· ½ cup dark brown sugar
· ½ large lime, juiced (about 1 tablespoon)
· ½ large garlic clove, peeled, grated (about ½ teaspoon)
· ¼ teaspoon red pepper flakes
· 1 lime, cut into four wedges

[Z] Substitute ¼ cup plus 1 tablespoon Stevia in the Raw® (or favorite no-calorie sweetener).

Coconut Rice
· 1 mango, skinned, cut into 4 pieces
· 1 tablespoon olive oil
· ½ tablespoon yellow onion, finely chopped
· ¼ large garlic clove, peeled, grated (about ¼ teaspoon)
· 1 cup jasmine rice, rinsed
· ¾ cup coconut milk
· ¼ teaspoon kosher salt
· ½ medium lime, juiced (about 2½ teaspoons)
· Zest of 1 large lime (about 2 teaspoons)

Garnishes
· Red pepper flakes, additional lime zest, cilantro leaves

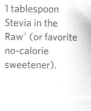

→ **WHERE TO BUY**
Find cachaça (ka-SHAH-sah), a Brazilian liquor distilled from sugarcane juice, in many liquor stores. Look for sugarcane swizzle sticks at amazon.com.

DIRECTIONS
Rinse the shrimp in cold water and pat them dry with paper towels. Using the point of a paring knife, poke a hole in each shrimp where it will be skewered with the sugarcane stick. Thread 5 to 6 shrimp onto each skewer. Set aside. *(Continued page 70)*

"Just the name 'caipirinha' had me longing to curl my toes in the warm South American sand and sway my hips." —CATHERINE

(Caipirinha-Glazed Shrimp Skewers, continued from page 68)

Caipirinha glaze. Combine the cachaça, brown sugar, lime juice, garlic and the ¼ teaspoon red pepper flakes in a small nonreactive saucepan over high heat. Stir and bring the mixture to a boil. Reduce to medium heat and simmer until the liquid thickens and is reduced by half, about 8 minutes. This glaze will not be as syrupy as a traditional glaze. Season with salt. Remove from heat and set aside.

Shrimp. Spray the grill with nonstick cooking spray or coat with oil. Heat the grill at high. Season the shrimp with salt and pepper. Using a basting brush, brush the shrimp on both sides with the glaze. Place the skewered shrimp on the grill grate over direct heat. Grill them for 2 to 3 minutes each side, basting with glaze 2 to 3 times during grilling. Shrimp are done when they are firm and opaque white. Remove from the grill and squeeze the juice of 1 lime wedge over each skewer.

Coconut rice. Grill the mango segments for about 2 minutes on each side. Baste with caipirinha glaze while cooking. Remove from heat and dice. Set aside. Heat the olive oil over medium-high heat in a medium, heavy-bottomed saucepan. Add the onion and garlic and sauté until fragrant and translucent, about 3 to 5 minutes. Add the rice and stir to coat the grains with oil. Stir in ¾ cup water, coconut milk and salt and bring to a boil. Stir again, reduce the heat, cover the pot and simmer for 15 minutes. Remove the pot from heat and leave covered for 5 minutes more. Uncover, fluff the rice with a fork and add the lime juice, zest and mangoes.

To plate. Divide the rice evenly among 4 plates. Place a shrimp skewer on top of the rice. Sprinkle red pepper flakes and lime zest over the shrimp and rice and garnish with fresh cilantro.

Per serving 470 calories, 9 grams total fat, 3 grams saturated fat, 3 grams monounsaturated fat, 1 gram polyunsaturated fat, 170 milligrams cholesterol, 60 grams carbohydrates, 2 grams fiber, 27 grams protein, 180 milligrams sodium

LOUISIANA-INSPIRED SHRIMP & SAUSAGE RICE BOWL

MORVEN WALKER OF MANAWATU, NEW ZEALAND

THIS ONE-POT MEAL CAN BE COOKED ON THE STOVE, IN A RICE COOKER OR ALL DAY IN A SLOW COOKER.

MAKES 4 SERVINGS | TOTAL PREP/COOK TIME: 30 MINUTES

★★☆

INGREDIENTS

· 2 tablespoons olive oil
· 1 medium white onion, peeled, chopped (about 1 cup)
· 3 medium celery ribs, sliced (about 1 cup)
· 1 large green bell pepper, seeded, deveined, chopped (about 1 cup)
· 1 medium garlic clove, peeled, minced (about 1 teaspoon)
· ½ pound smoked sausage, diced
· 1 (14.5-ounce) can diced tomatoes
· 1 bay leaf
· 1 teaspoon oregano
· 1 teaspoon paprika
· Coarse salt and freshly ground pepper
· 1 cup uncooked brown rice
· 2 cups homemade or prepared low-sodium chicken broth
· ½ pound large shrimp, peeled, deveined (15-18)
· Hot sauce (optional)
· Chopped fresh parsley (optional)

DIRECTIONS

Heat the olive oil in a skillet over medium-high heat. Add the onion, celery and pepper to the pan and cook until the vegetables are soft, about 5 minutes. Stir in the garlic and sausage. Pour in the tomatoes. Place the bay leaf into the pan. Season with oregano, paprika, salt and pepper. Add the rice and chicken broth and bring to a boil. Reduce the heat to medium low. Cover the pan with a lid. Add the shrimp during the last 5 minutes of cooking. Season with hot sauce and garnish with fresh parsley if desired.

....

Per serving 557 calories, 27 grams total fat, 8 grams saturated fat, 14 grams monounsaturated fat, 4 grams polyunsaturated fat, 127 milligrams cholesterol, 50 grams carbohydrates, 4 grams fiber, 27 grams protein, 1,041 milligrams sodium

➤ GO LEANER

Substitute a light chicken sausage instead of the smoked sausage to save about 90 calories, 12 grams of total fat and 4 grams of saturated fat per serving.

ASIAN TURKEY BURGERS

FROM LAURA GUION OF CONNECTICUT, USA

SERVE ON A WHOLE-GRAIN BUN AND ADD FAVORITE TOPPERS SUCH AS SLICED TOMATOES, RED ONION, AVOCADO OR GRILLED PINEAPPLE.

MAKES 4 SERVINGS | TOTAL PREP/COOK TIME: 20 MINUTES

★ ★ ★

INGREDIENTS

· 1 pound ground turkey
· 2-3 green onions, thinly sliced (about ¼ cup)
· 1 tablespoon low-sodium soy sauce
· 1-inch piece fresh ginger, peeled, grated (about 1 tablespoon)
· 2 medium garlic cloves, peeled, minced (about 2 teaspoons)
· 1 large egg white, beaten
· Coarse salt and freshly ground pepper

DIRECTIONS

Place the ground turkey into a large bowl. Add the onions, soy sauce, ginger, garlic and egg. Season with salt and pepper. Use your hands to gently mix together all of the ingredients. Form into 4 patties. Coat a grill pan with vegetable oil spray and heat over medium-high heat. Grill the patties, turning once, until a thermometer inserted into the center reaches 170°, about 6 to 8 minutes.

....

Per serving 185 calories, 9 grams total fat, 3 grams saturated fat, 4 grams monounsaturated fat, 2 grams polyunsaturated fat, 90 milligrams cholesterol, 21 grams protein, 25 grams carbohydrates, 0 grams fiber, 241 milligrams sodium

➡ **MAKE IT A MEAL**
Add a garden salad with homemade ginger dressing or baked sweet potato fries.

LAURA'S STORY
EATING SMART

Years ago, when I worked for a health club, I was in really great shape. But after having a child and spending 10 years at a desk job, I had gained a lot of weight. I was the typical working mom, putting everybody else first and not taking time to do things—like exercise—for myself. At 190 pounds, I felt tired all the time and was pretty discouraged when trying on clothes or looking at myself in photos. This wasn't my perception of *me* at all.

I decided to try a Zumba class and had a ton of fun. Now I'm hooked. The stress relief has been phenomenal, and I've lost 30 pounds so far!

Easy switches. My eating habits haven't changed much. I love to cook and bake, and I'm never going to give up something I really love. But I do want to get the most bang for my exercise buck! Here are a few little things that make a big difference for me:

➤ To change my sense of proportion, I eat meals off a salad plate rather than a large dinner plate and still feel full.

➤ I go for fat-free half-and-half in coffee and 1% milk in place of whole milk.

➤ Ground turkey is my fave substitute for ground beef.

➤ Brownies are a must-have. In the past, I'd have one (or more) every night. Now I enjoy a two-inch square on nights I've been to a Zumba class. It's my reward for busting all those calories on the dance floor!

A shift in thinking. I think more about my food choices now. After enjoying the benefits of losing weight, I don't want to blow it! I'm finally getting my body back and having an amazing time doing it.

IN THE KNOW

Picadillo. Similar to hash, picadillo *(pee-kah-DEE-yoh)* is popular in many Latin American countries. Though traditionally made with ground beef and tomatoes, this turkey variation is true to the dish's name, which comes from the Spanish verb "picar," meaning to finely chop.

Chayote. Although native to Mexico, the chayote *(chahy-OH-teh)* fruit has made its way to grocery stores worldwide. It tastes like a cross between a cucumber and a potato and can be prepared like summer squash. Substitute with a rutabaga or a parsnip.

Salsa Lizano. Salsa Lizano *(lee-SAHN-oh)* is a mild Costa Rican sauce used in many Latin dishes and can be found online or in grocery stores carrying Latin American foods. You can substitute with steak sauce or Worcestershire sauce or a combination of both.

TURKEY PICADILLO
FROM LISA VALLEJOS OF CALIFORNIA, USA

HEARTY MEETS HEALTHY IN THIS SIMPLY DELICIOUS STEW.

MAKES 6 SERVINGS | *TOTAL PREP/COOK TIME: 40 MINUTES*
★★★

INGREDIENTS
· 1 tablespoon olive oil
· 1 medium onion, peeled, finely diced (about 1 cup)
· 1 medium garlic clove, peeled, minced (about 1 teaspoon)
· 1 pound ground turkey (dark and white meat)
· Coarse salt and freshly ground pepper
· 1 small chayote squash, peeled, seeded, finely diced (about 1½ cups)
· 1 large russet potato, peeled, finely diced (about 1½ cups)
· 1 large zucchini, finely diced (about 2 cups)
· ½ cup Salsa Lizano

DIRECTIONS
Heat the olive oil in a pan over medium-high heat. Add the onion and garlic and cook until soft, about 3 minutes. Add the ground turkey to the pan. Season with salt and pepper. Cook until browned and crumbly, about 10 minutes. Add the chayote squash and potato and cook for 10 minutes more. Add the zucchini and stir in the Salsa Lizano. Cover and cook for 5 minutes more.

....

Per serving 191 calories, 9 grams total fat, 2 grams saturated fat, 4 grams monounsaturated fat, 2 grams polyunsaturated fat, 60 milligrams cholesterol, 13 grams carbohydrates, 2 grams fiber, 15 grams protein, 170 milligrams sodium

"This one-skillet meal reminds me of gatherings with my husband's family in Costa Rica." —LISA

SWEET & SASSY MARINATED BEEF

FROM CELESTE BURG OF PENNSYLVANIA, USA

UNCORK A BOTTLE OF WINE AND SERVE THIS ELEGANT ENTRÉE BY CANDLELIGHT.

MAKES 4 SERVINGS | TOTAL PREP/COOK TIME: 30 MINUTES PLUS 2-3 HOURS TO MARINATE

★★☆

INGREDIENTS

· 1 pound flank steak, sirloin or other cut of beef

Marinade

· 6 ounces low-sodium soy sauce
· 1 tablespoon sherry
· ½ tablespoon brown sugar
· ¾ teaspoon ground ginger
· ¾ teaspoon dry mustard
· 2 garlic cloves, chopped (about 2 teaspoons)
· 2 whole garlic cloves, peeled
· 1 teaspoon chili sauce
· Parsley for garnish (optional)
· Horseradish for garnish (optional)

DIRECTIONS

Whisk the marinade ingredients together and place the meat and marinade in a sealable plastic bag (such as Ziploc®). Seal and marinate several hours in the refrigerator. Place the marinated meat on a broiler pan coated with vegetable oil and discard the leftover marinade. Broil in the oven 9 to 12 minutes, turning once with tongs. Do not over-cook. Slice and place on a serving platter. If desired, garnish with parsley and serve with horseradish.

....

Per serving 300 calories, 15 grams total fat, 6 grams saturated fat, 6 grams monounsaturated fat, 0 grams polyunsaturated fat, 60 milligrams cholesterol, 4 grams carbohydrates, 0 grams fiber, 34 grams protein, 520 milligrams sodium

MEATY CHILI

FROM KERI SMITH OF NEW YORK, USA

THIS ONE'S SO VERSATILE! ADD HOT PEPPER SAUCE. TRY BEANS INSTEAD OF BEEF. EXPERIMENT WITH DIFFERENT GARNISHES.

MAKES 6 SERVINGS | TOTAL PREP/COOK TIME: 25 MINUTES PLUS 2 HOURS TO SIMMER 🌶

★★☆

INGREDIENTS

· 1 tablespoon olive oil
· 1½ pounds 90% lean ground beef
· 1 medium white onion, peeled, diced (about 1 cup)
· 1 large red bell pepper, seeded, deveined, diced (about 1 cup)
· 5 medium garlic cloves, peeled, minced (about 1½-2 tablespoons)
· 1 (28-ounce) can crushed tomatoes
· 1½ tablespoons tomato paste
· 3 tablespoons chili powder
· 2 teaspoons ground cumin
· ½ teaspoon ground cinnamon
· ½ teaspoon cayenne pepper
· 1 dried bay leaf
· 2 tablespoons chopped fresh basil
· Cooked brown rice (optional)
· Garnishes (optional): chopped green onions, diced avocado, shredded reduced-fat cheddar, light sour cream

DIRECTIONS

Heat the olive oil in a large, deep skillet or soup pot over medium-high heat. Brown the beef, breaking up large clumps, until cooked through, about 5 to 10 minutes. Stir in the onion, pepper and garlic. Pour in the crushed tomatoes and tomato paste. Stir in the dry spices. Simmer for 5 to 10 minutes. At this point, if the chili is too thick, you can add water to the pot to reach your desired consistency. Reduce the heat to low and simmer for 2 hours.

Stir in the fresh basil during the last 5 minutes of cooking. Discard the bay leaf. If desired, add cooked brown rice and favorite garnishes.

....

Per serving 350 calories, 20 grams total fat, 7 grams saturated fat, 9 grams monounsaturated fat, 1 gram polyunsaturated fat, 69 milligrams cholesterol, 19 grams carbohydrates, 6 grams fiber, 26 grams protein, 304 milligrams sodium

➜ **LEFTOVERS?**

Scoop up chili with a few home-baked tortilla chips for a filling midday snack.

HOMETOWN MEATLOAF

FROM JANINE KOUTSKY OF PENNSYLVANIA, USA

TRY THIS FRESH TWIST ON A COMFORT-FOOD CLASSIC. THE VEGGIES AND TOMATO SAUCE MAKE THE LOAF MOIST—A GOOD IDEA WHEN USING LEAN MEATS.

MAKES 8 SERVINGS | TOTAL PREP/COOK TIME: 1 HOUR, 30 MINUTES

★★☆

INGREDIENTS
Meatloaf
- 1 tablespoon canola oil
- ½ medium onion, minced (about ½ cup)
- 1 small stalk celery, finely chopped (about ⅓ cup)
- 2 slices whole-wheat bread, coarsely ground into crumbs (about ½ cup)
- ½ pound 90% lean ground beef
- ½ pound 99% lean ground turkey
- ¾ teaspoon salt
- ⅛ teaspoon black pepper
- 1 small carrot, shredded (about ⅓ cup)
- 2 egg whites
- ¼ cup tomato sauce

Sauce
- 1½ teaspoons brown sugar
- 1½ teaspoons yellow mustard
- 1½ teaspoons apple cider vinegar
- ¼ cup tomato sauce

DIRECTIONS
Meatloaf. Preheat the oven to 350°. Warm the oil in a skillet over medium-high heat, add the onion and celery and stir-fry about 5 minutes. Remove the skillet from heat. In a separate bowl, combine breadcrumbs, beef, turkey, salt, pepper, carrot, egg whites and tomato sauce. Add the cooled onion and celery and mix with spoon until all ingredients are combined. Place the meat mixture into a 9 x 5-inch loaf pan and shape.

Sauce. Place all of the sauce ingredients in a bowl and whisk to combine. Spread sauce over top of meatloaf. Bake at 350° until internal temperature reaches 165°, about 50 minutes.

. . . .

Per serving 140 calories, 7 grams total fat, 2 grams saturated fat, 3 grams monounsaturated fat, 1 gram polyunsaturated fat, 40 milligrams cholesterol, 7 grams carbohydrates, less than 1 gram fiber, 13 grams protein, 420 milligrams sodium

MAKING BREADCRUMBS

To avoid stale-tasting crumbs, use fresh, dry bread. If bread is too spongy to crumble, first place slices on an ungreased baking sheet and bake in a 300° oven for 10 minutes, turning once. Remove from the oven and cool. Tear bread into pieces and place in the bowl of a food processor. Pulse until coarsely ground crumbs are formed. Make extra breadcrumbs and store in an airtight container for future use.

SLOW-COOKER BEEF

FROM CATHERINE DE ORIO OF ILLINOIS, USA
EDITOR-IN-CHIEF, CULINARYCURATOR.COM &
GLAMOURGRUB.COM

THIS DELECTABLE POT ROAST IS A REAL TIME SAVER!
IT TAKES ONLY MINUTES TO ASSEMBLE AND CAN BE LEFT IN
THE SLOW COOKER ALL DAY.

MAKES 4 SERVINGS | TOTAL PREP/COOK TIME: 15 MINUTES
PLUS 4-9 HOURS IN SLOW COOKER
★★☆

→ GO HOTTER
For a spicier dish, leave in the jalapeño pepper seeds.

→ CUT THE SALT
Save about 480 milligrams of sodium per serving by using only 1 teaspoon of kosher salt.

INGREDIENTS
· 1 (2- to 3-pound) eye of round roast (or substitute a leaner cut of beef)
· 2 teaspoons kosher salt
· 2 teaspoons ground cumin
· 1 teaspoon dried oregano
· ¼ teaspoon freshly ground black pepper
· 1 bay leaf
· 1 (14.5-ounce) can low-sodium diced tomatoes
· 1 medium onion, peeled, quartered (about 1 cup)
· 2 medium carrots, peeled, trimmed, cut into 1-inch-thick slices (about 1 cup)
· 2 medium jalapeño peppers, seeded, deveined, chopped (about ¼ cup)
· 1 bell pepper, seeded, deveined, cut into strips (about 1 cup)

DIRECTIONS
Spray the inside of a slow cooker with nonstick spray. Place the eye of round inside the slow cooker. Season with salt, cumin, oregano and pepper. Add the bay leaf. In the following order, add the tomatoes, onion, carrots, jalapeños and bell pepper. Cover and cook 8 to 9 hours on low heat or about 4 hours on high heat, until meat is tender. Serve with brown rice.

....

Per serving 330 calories, 6 grams total fat, 2 grams saturated fat, 2.5 grams monounsaturated fat, 0 grams polyunsaturated fat, 80 milligrams cholesterol, 14 grams carbohydrates, 4 grams fiber, 53 grams protein, 1,047 milligrams sodium

"This dish is perfect for a cool-weather evening." —CATHERINE

THAI CURRIED VEGETABLES

FROM CARRIE ELLINGSON OF ALBERTA, CANADA

THIS AROMATIC DISH MORPHS INTO A MEAL WHEN SERVED OVER RICE OR NOODLES.

MAKES 4 SERVINGS | TOTAL PREP/COOK TIME: 40 MINUTES Ⅴ 🌶
★ ★ ☆

→ **GO Leaner**
Use light coconut milk in place of regular to save 170 calories, 17 grams of total fat and 15 grams of saturated fat per serving.

→ **Make IT a meal**
Add cubes of firm tofu, chicken or fish to the wok.

INGREDIENTS
· 1 (13.5-ounce) can coconut milk
· 2 tablespoons low-sodium soy sauce
· 1½ tablespoons natural brown sugar
· 1½ teaspoons curry powder
· 1-2 teaspoons red Thai curry paste
· 1 pound fresh broccoli florets (about 2 cups)
· 1 large bell pepper, seeded, deveined, chopped (about 1 cup)
· 2 medium carrots, peeled, trimmed, sliced (about 1 cup)
· 1 pint cherry tomatoes, halved (about 1 cup)
· 4 ounces button mushrooms, sliced (about 1 cup)
· 1 bunch green onions, thinly sliced (about 1 cup)
· 2 medium garlic cloves, peeled, minced (about 2 teaspoons)
· Coarse salt and freshly ground pepper
· 2 tablespoons chopped fresh basil

[Z] Substitute 1½ tablespoons Stevia in the Raw® (or favorite no-calorie sweetener).

DIRECTIONS
Pour the coconut milk into a wok (or large skillet) over medium-high heat. Stir in the soy sauce, sugar, curry powder and curry paste. Cook for 3 minutes. Add the veggies to the wok. Cook until the veggies are crisp-tender, about 15 minutes. Season with salt and pepper. Garnish with basil.

Per serving 339 calories, 25 grams total fat, 20 grams saturated fat, 1 gram monounsaturated fat, 1 gram polyunsaturated fat, 0 milligrams cholesterol, 28 grams carbohydrates, 10 grams fiber, 8 grams protein, 367 milligrams sodium

CARRIE'S STORY
A FRESH START

Although I took dance classes as a kid, I'd been overweight most of my life. By age 30, I found myself out of breath when doing the simplest things and could no longer do the job I loved—caring for horses. It was time for a lifestyle change.

A friend and I tried a Zumba class together and fell in love with it. It got me back into dancing and also made me want to try other activities—like spinning—that I never would have tried before.

So far, I've lost 45 pounds without resorting to crazy diets! None of my old clothes fit, and I feel like a new person. Here are my favorite nutrition tips for fellow Zumba lovers:

➤ ***Mama was right—you are what you eat.*** Use the freshest whole foods you can find to give your body the nutrients it needs.

➤ ***Keep it simple.*** Always have healthy ingredients on hand and basic recipes you can whip up on short notice. Having a repertoire of easy, healthful meals to make at home can keep you from reaching for packaged, processed foods that may be high in sodium and unhealthy fats. Save complicated recipes for special occasions when you can give them the attention they need.

➤ ***Eat everything.*** There isn't anything I tell myself I can't have in moderation. Acknowledging—rather than ignoring—cravings keeps me in control. I can eat a small amount of what I crave and stay on the healthy path I've chosen.

➤ ***Explore cuisines from other cultures and countries.*** I love to cook for family and friends, and one of my passions is personalizing recipes. Most of my favorite foods draw on different ethnic flavors, but adding my own twist keeps it interesting!

SPICY NOODLE STIR-FRY

FROM KIM LEVETT OF SUFFOLK, UK

YOU'LL LOVE THE COMBINATION OF HEAT AND SWEET! A WOK IS THE IDEAL TOOL TO PREPARE THIS DISH, BUT A LARGE SKILLET WORKS, TOO.

MAKES 4 SERVINGS | TOTAL PREP/COOK TIME: 25 MINUTES

★★★

→ **NO FRESH PASTA?**

Substitute soba noodles or cooked dry pasta.

→ **NO FRESH CHILES?**

Dried chiles work, too. If you love spicier food, add more.

INGREDIENTS

· 8 ounces fresh egg noodles
· 2 tablespoons unsalted crunchy peanut butter
· 2 tablespoons sesame oil
· 2 tablespoons sweet chili sauce
· 1 tablespoon low-sodium soy sauce
· 1 large lime, juiced (about 2 tablespoons)
· 1 tablespoon olive oil
· 2 boneless, skinless chicken breasts, cut into strips
· 1 bunch green onions, thinly sliced (about 1 cup)
· 1 large, fresh red chile, seeded, deveined, chopped
  (about 2 tablespoons) (for a spicier dish, include a few seeds)
· ¾ cup baby sweet corn
· ¾ cup snow peas
· 2 tablespoons pine nuts

DIRECTIONS

Bring a pot of salted water to a boil over medium-high heat. Cook the noodles al dente, about 3 to 5 minutes. Drain.

Whisk together crunchy peanut butter, sesame oil, chili sauce, soy sauce and lime juice. Heat the olive oil in a skillet (or wok) over medium-high heat. Cook the chicken strips until golden, about 5 minutes. Add the green onions, red chile, sweet corn and snow peas. Cook until the veggies are crisp-tender, about 4 minutes. Stir in the sauce. Add the noodles and toss until all of the ingredients are evenly coated. Sprinkle with pine nuts.

....

Per serving 532 calories, 21 grams total fat, 4 grams saturated fat, 9 grams monounsaturated fat, 7 grams polyunsaturated fat, 106 milligrams cholesterol, 55 grams carbohydrates, 5 grams fiber, 32 grams protein, 213 milligrams sodium

KIM'S STORY
COMMON-SENSE ADVICE

As a Zumba instructor, I impress on my students the importance of a balanced diet and regular exercise. As a mom, I try to practice what I preach, serving my sons a variety of fruits, vegetables, carbs and protein at every meal.

Before and after. Breakfast is essential. The kids and I sit down at the table as often as time allows, eating porridge, cereal, granola or yogurt. Before a Zumba class, I eat a banana and take along a small container of dried fruit and nuts or a protein shake so I'm not tempted by unhealthy quick-fix snacks after a workout.

I also make sure meals, like this Spicy Noodle Stir-Fry, contain veggies, carbs and protein so I get all the vital nutrients needed to help restore glycogen to the muscles and repair them after exercise. Then I'm ready to give 100 percent to my next day's workout!

Visible results. At the age of 43, my body has never been in better shape! To stay motivated, I tack a photo of me—looking my most fantastic—on the fridge door. It's a tried-and-true way to make health and fitness my priority.

PASTA WITH PROSCIUTTO & GREENS

FROM SOCCORO SEPULCHRE OF NEW SOUTH WALES, AUSTRALIA

COOKING THE GARLIC IN THE OIL IS A POWERFUL FLAVOR BOOSTER.

MAKES 4 SERVINGS | TOTAL PREP/COOK TIME: 20 MINUTES

★★☆

INGREDIENTS

· 8 ounces spaghetti pasta
· ½ cup chopped fresh basil
· ¼ cup chopped fresh parsley
· ¼ cup chopped fresh mint
· 1 tablespoon chopped fresh oregano
· 3 ounces prosciutto, about 5 thin slices, diced
· ¼ cup olive oil
· 6 large garlic cloves, peeled, crushed (about 2 tablespoons)
· 4 ounces Parmesan cheese, shaved (about 1 cup)
· Freshly ground pepper

DIRECTIONS

Bring a pot of salted water to a boil over medium-high heat. Cook the pasta al dente, about 10 minutes. Drain and pour into a large bowl. Place the herbs and prosciutto on top of the pasta. Heat the olive oil in a skillet over medium heat. Add the garlic and cook until it begins to turn golden, about 2 minutes. Use a slotted spoon to remove the garlic from the oil. Pour the warm oil over the pasta. Add the cheese and toss to combine. Season with pepper.

....

Per serving 537 calories, 25 grams total fat, 8 grams saturated fat, 13 grams monounsaturated fat, 2 grams polyunsaturated fat, 37 milligrams cholesterol, 52 grams carbohydrates, 6 grams fiber, 27 grams protein, 1,113 milligrams sodium

➜ GO LEANER

Cut the Parmesan in half to save 50 calories, 3.5 grams of total fat and 2 grams of saturated fat per serving.

➜ REDUCE THE SODIUM

For a lower-sodium, vegetarian side dish, skip the salty prosciutto and Parmesan, and sprinkle on a little salt or a low-sodium cheese alternative such as Parma!™ from Sister River Foods, found online.

"The mint in this dish gives it a refreshing kick! I pair the pasta with a fresh papaya salad to make it a meal." —SOCCORO

GNOCCHI, SPINACH & BEANS

FROM MEREDITH ELLIS OF NEW YORK, USA

THIS MEATLESS MEAL REALLY SATISFIES. IT'S SUPERFAST AND EASY TO MAKE AFTER A WEEKNIGHT ZUMBA CLASS.

MAKES 4 SERVINGS | TOTAL PREP/COOK TIME: 15 MINUTES **V**

★ ★ ☆

INGREDIENTS
· 1 (8-ounce) package whole-wheat gnocchi
· 1 tablespoon olive oil
· 1 medium garlic clove, peeled, minced (about 1 teaspoon)
· 1 pound fresh spinach leaves (about 4 cups)
· 1 (15.5-ounce) can pink beans, drained, rinsed (or substitute kidney beans)
· Coarse salt and freshly ground pepper
· 2 tablespoons grated Parmesan cheese for garnish (or substitute nutritional yeast for a vegan or lower-sodium dish)

DIRECTIONS
Cook the gnocchi in boiling salted water according to the directions on the package. While the gnocchi is cooking, heat the olive oil in a skillet over medium heat. Add the garlic and cook until soft, about 1 minute. Raise heat to medium high, add the spinach and toss until wilted, about 5 minutes. Stir in the beans with ¼ cup of the water used to boil the gnocchi. Heat 2 to 3 minutes. Drain the cooked gnocchi and add it to the skillet, mixing with the beans. Season with salt and pepper. Garnish with Parmesan cheese.

....

Per serving 280 calories, 5 grams total fat, 1 gram saturated fat, 2.5 grams monounsaturated fat, .5 gram polyunsaturated fat, 2 milligrams cholesterol, 45 grams carbohydrates, 8 grams fiber, 12 grams protein, 636 milligrams sodium

➤ **"a" FOR THE EYES**
The spinach here provides 210% of the recommended daily intake for vitamin A, which can help keep eyes healthy.

➤ **GO LEANER**
To reduce fat, skip the oil and heat the garlic in a nonstick skillet. Add the spinach and a couple spritzes of water, cover and steam.

LASAGNA MUFFINS

INSPIRED BY A RECIPE FROM DAYANA KIBILDS OF PENNSYLVANIA, USA

THIS RICH DISH SATISFIES IN JUST A FEW BITES, AND YOU CAN CUSTOMIZE INGREDIENTS TO PLEASE DIFFERENT DINNER GUESTS!

MAKES 12 SERVINGS | TOTAL PREP/COOK TIME: 1 HOUR, 10 MINUTES PLUS TIME TO COOL

★★☆

INGREDIENTS

· 2 tablespoons olive oil
· 1 medium white onion, peeled, chopped (about 1 cup)
· 2 medium garlic cloves, peeled, minced (about 2 teaspoons) (or substitute chopped, roasted garlic from a jar)
· 1 pound lean ground turkey breast (or substitute 90% lean ground beef or favorite vegetarian ground beef replacement, *see page 84*)
· ½ teaspoon paprika
· ¾ teaspoon dried basil
· ½ teaspoon ground oregano
· Salt and freshly ground pepper
· 1 (28-ounce) can crushed tomatoes
· ½ teaspoon crushed red pepper flakes (or more for a spicier sauce)
· 8 ounces part-skim ricotta (about 1 cup) (or substitute tofu ricotta, *see page 84*)
· 3 ounces low-fat, low-sodium sliced ham (about 5 slices), diced (or substitute finely chopped mushrooms in a vegetarian version)
· 2 ounces Parmesan cheese, grated (about ½ cup), divided (or substitute vegan Parmesan, such as low-sodium Parma!™ brand, or nutritional yeast, *see page 84*)
· 36 wonton wrappers (or 12 egg-roll wrappers)
· 1 teaspoon cornstarch (optional, for assembling egg-roll wrappers, see *"Method 2," page 84*)
· 4 ounces reduced-fat mozzarella cheese, grated (about 1 cup) (or substitute nondairy mozzarella, *see page 84*)

DIRECTIONS

Preheat the oven to 375°. Heat the olive oil in a large pot over medium heat. Add the onion and garlic to the oil. Cook for 2 minutes. Add the turkey to the pan. Season with paprika, basil, oregano, salt and pepper. Cook the mixture, stirring to break up any clumps, until the turkey is lightly browned, about 6 minutes. Stir in the crushed tomatoes, 1 cup water and crushed red pepper. Increase the heat to bring the sauce to a low boil. When it starts to bubble, reduce the heat to medium low and cook for 20 minutes.

Combine the ricotta, ham and 2 tablespoons Parmesan in a bowl and mix until smooth. *(Continued page 84)*

→ **VEG-FRIENDLY OPTIONS**

Make vegan or vegetarian versions with the optional ingredients here and on page 84. Look for eggless wonton wrappers in some Asian and natural-foods markets—or search keywords "eggless wonton" online to find easy ways to make them yourself.

DAYANA'S STORY
THE DIETING DRAG

I'd been trying to lose weight since I was 13. The problem? I had a "diet" mentality. I'd lose pounds, end the diet and gain back all the weight. Here's what helped me drop—and keep off—50 pounds.

A little awareness goes a long way. When I was a kid, I wasn't allowed to leave the table until I'd eaten everything on my plate. My food portions had always been way too big. Imagine my shock when I started counting the calories!

Now I put less on the plate and eat more slowly so I can tell when I'm feeling full. If I have a meal that I know is higher in fat or calories, I compensate by eating lighter, nutrient-rich dishes the next few meals.

Eating less while eating more often can stave off hunger and help maintain a healthy weight. If I have a light salad for lunch and try to make it six hours to dinner, I'll be famished and overeat. So I eat three small-portion meals and two snacks—fruits, vegetables or yogurt—in between. It feels like I'm eating all the time, so I don't have cravings or go hungry.

Exercise is a must. This may sound crazy, but you know how some people set aside time to watch a favorite TV show? That's what I do with exercise. I see it as my indulgence. I used to hate working out, and now I'm a Zumba instructor, dancing seven hours a week!

GET CREATIVE!

If you love to experiment in the kitchen, try these veg-friendly alternatives to traditional lasagna.

▶ *Make tofu ricotta.* Squeeze liquid from 1 pound of firm tofu and crumble tofu into the bowl of a food processor. Add 1 teaspoon agave nectar, 1 teaspoon vinegar and 1 tablespoon lemon juice. Blend to a ricotta-like consistency.

▶ *Skip or replace the meat.* Crumbled tempeh, organic textured soy protein (such as Bob's Red Mill® brand) and prepared vegan crumbles (such as Boca® or Yves® brands) all have little to no saturated fat. Check labels to choose lower-sodium options.

▶ *Go for color and texture.* Mix any of these veggies into the ricotta: fresh or frozen chopped spinach (thawed and drained), shredded zucchini or summer squash, chopped broccoli florets, chopped mushrooms or grated carrots. Try cubed eggplant, cooked with the onions, in place of the ground turkey.

▶ *Use alternative sauces.* Instead of red sauce, try a spicy salsa, a light peanut sauce or a gingery carrot sauce.

▶ *Experiment with nondairy mozzarella.* Versions by Daiya™ Foods, Follow Your Heart® and Chicago Vegan Foods™—found online and in natural-foods markets—have little to no saturated fat. For recipes to make your own healthy versions, search "vegan mozzarella" online.

▶ *Try a vegan best-kept secret.* Cheesy-tasting nutritional yeast—not to be confused with baker's or brewer's yeast—is a healthy lower-sodium, nondairy alternative to Parmesan.

(Lasagna Muffins, continued from page 82)

Assembly. To assemble the muffins, spray a 12-cup muffin pan with vegetable oil spray. Remove wonton or egg-roll wrappers from their packaging and cover them with a damp towel to keep them from drying out. Use one or all of the following building methods for an impressive presentation.

METHOD 1: OPEN-TOP LASAGNA MUFFIN

1. Press a wonton wrapper into the bottom of each cup and smooth against the sides. The corners should point up.
2. Position a second wrapper, turned 45° as shown, press into the bottom and smooth against the sides.
3. Add a spoonful of the turkey mixture, pressing with the spoon to cover the bottom. Spread a spoonful of the ricotta mixture on top. Sprinkle on 1 to 1½ teaspoons Parmesan.
4. Add a third wonton wrapper, gently pressing it into the cheese and against the sides of the cup. The corners should point up and sit higher than the lip of the cup.
5. Add a spoonful each of the turkey and ricotta mixtures.

METHOD 2: CLOSED-TOP LASAGNA MUFFIN

1. In a small bowl, mix cornstarch into 1½ teaspoons cold water and stir until it forms a thin paste.
2. Press an egg-roll wrapper into the bottom of the cup and smooth against the sides, letting the corners fall outside the cup.
3. Press layers of the turkey and ricotta mixtures into the cup until heaping. Sprinkle on 1 to 1½ teaspoons Parmesan.
4. Fold each corner of the wrapper over the filling so that the corners overlap in the middle. With your finger, add a dab of cornstarch paste under the top corner to seal.

METHOD 3: LASAGNA PURSE

Follow instructions 2 and 3 for the closed-top muffin. Instead of folding in the corners, cinch the egg-roll wrapper around the filling, as shown, and leave corners pointing up. The wrapper tips will be brown and crunchy after baking.

Baking the muffins. Bake the muffins for 10 minutes. Remove the pan from the oven and top each muffin with mozzarella cheese. Bake again until the cheese is melted and golden, 10 to 15 minutes more. Let the muffins cool about 10 minutes. Use a knife to cut around the edges and carefully remove the muffins. While you *may* be able to eat these by hand, avoid "uh-oh" moments and eat them with a fork! If there is any remaining sauce, spoon it over the top.

....

Open-top muffin per serving 254 calories, 8.5 grams total fat, 3.5 grams saturated fat, 3 grams monounsaturated fat, 1 gram polyunsaturated fat, 47 milligrams cholesterol, 22 grams carbohydrates, 2 grams fiber, 22 grams protein, 617 milligrams sodium

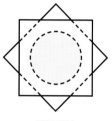

METHOD 1:
OPEN-TOP ASSEMBLY WITH
WONTON WRAPPER

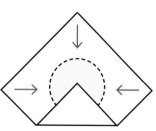

METHOD 2:
CLOSED-TOP ASSEMBLY
WITH EGG-ROLL WRAPPER

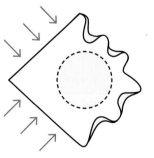

METHOD 3:
PURSE ASSEMBLY WITH
EGG-ROLL WRAPPER

Optional ingredients, building methods and illustrations by Ashley Pound

SPAGHETTI WITH CLAM SAUCE

FROM SHARYNE WOOD OF UTAH, USA

CANNED CLAMS WORK WELL IN THIS RECIPE, BUT GO FOR FRESH ONES IF YOU CAN FIND THEM IN YOUR AREA.

MAKES 6 SERVINGS | TOTAL PREP/COOK TIME: 30 MINUTES

★★☆

INGREDIENTS

· 1 tablespoon olive oil
· 4 medium garlic cloves, peeled, minced (about 1⅓ tablespoons)
· 1 (3.5-ounce) jar capers, drained, rinsed, liquid reserved
· 1 (28-ounce) can crushed tomatoes
· 4 (6.5-ounce) cans chopped clams
· 8 ounces mushrooms, sliced
· 2 tablespoons chopped fresh parsley
· Salt and freshly ground pepper
· 12 ounces whole-wheat spaghetti

DIRECTIONS

Heat the olive oil in a skillet over medium-high heat. Add the garlic and capers and cook until soft, about 2 minutes. Add the tomatoes, clams and 1 tablespoon reserved caper liquid. Add the mushrooms. Bring the sauce to a boil. Reduce the heat to medium low and cook until the liquid reduces by half, about 10 minutes. Stir in the parsley during the last few minutes of cooking. Season with salt and pepper.

Bring a pot of salted water to a boil over high heat. Add the pasta and cook al dente, about 10 to 12 minutes. Drain the pasta and add to the sauce.

....

Per serving 280 calories, 3.5 grams total fat, 0 grams saturated fat, 2 grams monounsaturated fat, 0 grams polyunsaturated fat, 5 milligrams cholesterol, 50 grams carbohydrates, 7 grams fiber, 14 grams protein, 887 milligrams sodium

SPAGHETTI SQUASH WITH MEAT SAUCE

FROM MORGAINE JENNINGS OF VERMONT, USA

LOADED WITH VITAMINS, SPAGHETTI SQUASH IS A LOW-CALORIE ALTERNATIVE TO WHEAT PASTA AND HAS FANTASTIC FLAVOR AND TEXTURE.

MAKES 6 SERVINGS | TOTAL PREP/COOK TIME: 40 MINUTES

★★☆

INGREDIENTS

· 1 large (4-pound) spaghetti squash
· 1 tablespoon olive oil
· 1 large yellow onion, peeled, finely diced (about 1½ cups)
· 3 medium carrots, peeled, trimmed, chopped (about 1½ cups)
· 3 medium garlic cloves, peeled, minced (about 1 tablespoon)
· 1 pound 90% lean ground beef
· Coarse salt and freshly ground pepper
· 1 (14-ounce) can diced tomatoes
· 1 tablespoon crushed red pepper flakes
· 1 teaspoon dried oregano
· 1 tablespoon chopped fresh basil
· Parmesan cheese, grated (optional)
· Crushed red pepper flakes for garnish (optional)

DIRECTIONS

Preheat the oven to 350°. Cut the spaghetti squash in half lengthwise. Spray the cut side of the squash with vegetable oil spray and place face down into a baking dish. Cook until the squash is tender, about 25 to 30 minutes.

Prepare the meat sauce by heating the olive oil in a skillet over medium-high heat. Add the onion and carrots and cook until soft, about 4 minutes. Add the garlic and cook about 1 minute. Add the beef and cook, stirring to break up large clumps, until browned, about 5 minutes more. Season with salt and pepper. Pour in the diced tomatoes. Stir in red pepper flakes, oregano and basil. Reduce the heat to medium low and cook for 10 minutes more.

Remove the squash from the oven. Set the squash standing up in a shallow bowl, holding it steady with one hand protected by a potholder. Use a fork to scrape out the pulp, which will look like spaghetti noodles. Discard the rind. Season the noodles with salt and pepper and top with the sauce. Garnish, if desired, with Parmesan cheese and additional crushed red pepper flakes.

....

Per serving 230 calories, 10 grams total fat, 3.5 grams saturated fat, 4.5 grams monounsaturated fat, 1 gram polyunsaturated fat, 50 milligrams cholesterol, 17 grams carbohydrates, 3 grams fiber, 17 grams protein, 220 milligrams sodium

➜ **MAKE IT YOUR OWN**
Adjust the amount of crushed red pepper flakes to control the heat.

For a vegetarian dish, skip the meat and add more vegetables. Chopped bell peppers or sliced mushrooms are tasty choices.

SHAKE 'N' DROP CHICKEN

INSPIRED BY A RECIPE FROM MICHELLE ENRIQUEZ OF NEVADA, USA

THIS IS IDEAL WHEN YOU'RE TAKING AN AFTERNOON ZUMBA CLASS. MARINATE THE CHICKEN BEFORE YOU GO AND PUT THE REST OF THE DISH TOGETHER WHEN YOU GET HOME.
MAKES 4 SERVINGS | TOTAL PREP/COOK TIME: 40 MINUTES PLUS 30 MINUTES TO MARINATE
★★☆

INGREDIENTS
· 2 large boneless, skinless chicken breasts (about 1½ pounds)
· 2 tablespoons olive oil
· Zest of 1 medium lemon (about 2 teaspoons)
· 1 medium lemon, juiced (about 3 tablespoons)
· 1 teaspoon Dijon-style mustard
· 1 teaspoon dried minced onion
· 1 teaspoon garlic powder
· Coarse salt and freshly ground pepper
· 1 large red bell pepper, seeded, deveined, sliced (about 1 cup)
· 1 medium onion, peeled, sliced (about 1 cup)
· 4 ounces fresh mushrooms, sliced (about 1 cup)
· 4 ounces fresh asparagus (about 16 medium spears), sliced (about 1 cup)
· 6 ounces reduced-fat cheddar cheese, shredded (about 1½ cups)

[Z] To further reduce the saturated fat, substitute a cheddar-style nondairy cheese that's made to melt, such as Teese by Chicago Vegan Foods™.

DIRECTIONS
Place the chicken breasts into a baking dish. In a bowl, whisk together the olive oil, lemon zest and juice, mustard, minced onion, garlic powder, salt and pepper. Pour the marinade over the chicken breasts, coating both sides. Cover and refrigerate for at least 30 minutes, up to 4 hours.

Preheat a grill pan coated with vegetable oil spray on medium-high heat. Remove the chicken from the marinade and discard the marinade. Grill the chicken, turning it once until it is cooked through, about 10 minutes, depending on the thickness of the breasts. Remove to a cutting board.

Add the bell pepper, onion, mushrooms and asparagus to the pan. Season with salt and pepper. Cook until the asparagus and bell pepper are crisp-tender, about 5 minutes. Remove the pan from the heat.

Preheat the oven to 350°. Slice the chicken breasts into 1-inch pieces and place into a baking pan. Cover the chicken with half of the cheese. Top the cheese with the vegetables. Top the vegetables with the remaining cheese. Place the dish into the oven and bake until the cheese melts, about 5 to 10 minutes.

....

Per serving 433 calories, 10 grams total fat, 6.5 grams saturated fat, 3 grams monounsaturated fat, 1 gram polyunsaturated fat, 80 milligrams cholesterol, 11 grams carbohydrates, 3 grams fiber, 52 grams protein, 385 milligrams sodium

CHICKEN, CHORIZO & CHICKPEA STEW

INSPIRED BY A RECIPE FROM JEANNETTE ELLIOTT OF GLOUCESTERSHIRE, UK

PREP THIS EASY STEW IN THE MORNING AND LET IT COOK ALL DAY IN A SLOW COOKER—OR MAKE IT JUST BEFORE DINNERTIME.

MAKES 6 SERVINGS | TOTAL PREP/COOK TIME: 40 MINUTES

★★☆

INGREDIENTS

- 2 tablespoons canola oil, divided
- 2 (4- to 6-ounce) boneless, skinless chicken breasts
- ½ teaspoon paprika
- ¼ teaspoon cumin
- ½ teaspoon garlic powder
- Coarse salt and freshly ground pepper
- 1 large yellow onion, peeled, finely diced (about 1½ cups)
- 8 ounces reduced-sodium soy chorizo sausage (see sidebar) (or substitute chicken chorizo)
- 3 cloves garlic, peeled, minced (about 1 tablespoon)
- 1 (14.5-ounce) can low-sodium diced tomatoes
- 1 (15.5-ounce) can chickpeas, drained, rinsed
- 1 teaspoon red pepper flakes

DIRECTIONS

In a small bowl, mix together the paprika, cumin and garlic powder. Heat 1 tablespooon oil in a large nonstick skillet over medium-high heat. Add the chicken and sprinkle the spice mixture evenly over the top. Season with salt and pepper. Cook, turning once, until both sides are golden, about 4 minutes. Remove the chicken to a cutting board.

Reduce heat to medium. Add 1 tablespoon oil and the onion to the skillet. Cook about 3 minutes, stirring the onions until soft. Raise the heat to medium high and add the chorizo and garlic, stirring to cook evenly, about 4 minutes (avoid overcooking, as this can dry out soy chorizo).

Pour in the tomatoes and the chickpeas (or transfer to a slow cooker for all-day cooking). Add the red pepper flakes. Season with salt and pepper. Bring the stew to a boil. Reduce the heat to medium low. Cut the chicken into 1-inch pieces and add to the skillet. Cook for 10 to 15 minutes.

....

Per serving 339 calories, 11 grams total fat, 1 gram saturated fat, 5.5 grams monounsaturated fat, 3.5 grams polyunsaturated fat, 41 milligrams cholesterol, 36 grams carbohydrates, 10 grams fiber, 24 grams protein, 435 milligrams sodium

SPICE IT UP!

Traditional pork chorizo is high in saturated fat, so we've used spicy soy chorizo, which has up to 80% less fat, less saturated fat and lots of flavor.

➤ Where to find it. Brands such as Cacique® Soy Chorizo and Yves® Veggie Chorizo are also lower in sodium. Find them—along with other tasty options—on the web and in some natural-foods markets and groceries. To make your own, search "soy chorizo" online and find lots of easy, healthful recipes.

➤ How to prepare it. Unlike the pork version, which can be sliced, soy chorizo has the consistency of ground meat. Cut off a segment of the chorizo, cut lengthwise through the casing and drop the "meat" directly into a skillet or pot.

CHICKEN STUFFED WITH SUN-DRIED TOMATOES, SPINACH & ARTICHOKE HEARTS

FROM CAREY PLOWMAN OF TENNESSEE, USA

THE CHEESY FILLING IN THIS DISH OVERFLOWS INTO THE PAN, BAKING IN AND AROUND THE CHICKEN. YUM! SERVE WITH WILD RICE OR QUINOA FOR A COMPLETE MEAL.

MAKES 4 SERVINGS | *TOTAL PREP/COOK TIME: 1 HOUR*

★★☆

INGREDIENTS

· 4 (4- to 6-ounce) boneless, skinless chicken breasts
· ¾ cup frozen chopped spinach, thawed, pressed through colander to remove excess liquid
· ½ cup reduced-fat ricotta cheese
· ½ cup chopped marinated artichoke hearts
· ½ cup sun-dried tomatoes in oil, drained, chopped
· 2 tablespoons grated Parmesan cheese (or substitute a lower-sodium Parmesan alternative such as Parma!™)
· ½ teaspoon garlic powder
· Coarse salt and freshly ground pepper
· 2 tablespoons olive oil

DIRECTIONS

Preheat the oven to 400°. Place the chicken breasts onto your work surface. Make a pocket in each breast by cutting a 2-inch-wide horizontal slit into the thickest part.

Combine the spinach, ricotta cheese, artichoke hearts, sun-dried tomatoes, Parmesan cheese and garlic powder in a bowl. Place ¼ of the filling into each of the chicken breasts. The filling will likely overflow from the breast into the pan.

Season the chicken with salt and pepper. Place into a baking dish. Drizzle the chicken with olive oil. Bake until the chicken is cooked through, about 30 to 40 minutes.

....

Per serving 290 calories, 13 grams total fat, 3 grams saturated fat, 6 grams monounsaturated fat, 1 gram polyunsaturated fat, 77 milligrams cholesterol, 10 grams carbohydrates, 2 grams fiber, 33 grams protein, 417 milligrams sodium

CAREY'S STORY
PAST THE PLATEAU

Being overweight most of my life, I had tried all kinds of diets, but nothing worked. I would start on Monday and bail out by Thursday. When it came to exercise, I was just "phoning it in" until I was introduced to Zumba dancing. Since then, the only thing I've gained is rhythm!

In addition to my classes, what helped me lose 42 pounds was keeping a food journal. Until I sat down and wrote out what I ate on a normal day, I had no idea how much I was actually consuming.

Here are a few favorite tips:
➤ *Feel fuller.* Load more vegetables into sandwiches and salads.
➤ *Make healthy substitutions.* Try hummus with pita instead of flatbread; salsa with home-baked tortilla chips instead of the fried, high-sodium variety; whole-wheat pasta instead of the white stuff; applesauce instead of oil in baking; olive oil instead of butter for sautéing.
➤ *Don't go "cold turkey."* It's too easy to binge when you don't indulge a few cravings. Enjoying a special treat at the end of the week keeps me on track toward my health and fitness goals.

As I aim to lose 30 more pounds, I still hit occasional walls. But by paying attention to my body and making changes gradually, I learn new things about myself every day.

SPINACH & PROSCIUTTO CHICKEN ROLLS

FROM CORY SAWYER OF NEW YORK, USA

THIS DELICIOUS DISH IS ELEGANT ENOUGH TO SERVE GUESTS. ADD A SIDE OF FRESH GREEN BEANS, STEAMED AND TOSSED WITH OLIVE OIL AND LEMON JUICE.

MAKES 4 SERVINGS | TOTAL PREP/COOK TIME: 45 MINUTES

★★☆

INGREDIENTS
· 4 (4-ounce) boneless, skinless chicken breasts
· Coarse salt and freshly ground pepper
· 4 tablespoons whole-wheat flour, divided
· 2 (1-ounce) slices reduced-fat Swiss cheese, cut in half
· 4 (1-ounce) slices prosciutto
· ¼ pound fresh baby spinach leaves (about 1 cup or add more if desired)
· 2 tablespoons olive oil (or substitute Earth Balance® buttery spread with olive oil for a buttery flavor)
· 1 tablespoon half-and-half
· 1 cup homemade or prepared low-sodium chicken broth

[Z] For a no-cholesterol alternative, try making a nondairy Swiss from scratch. Search keywords "nondairy Swiss cheese" online to find creative recipes using cashews, agar-agar and natural flavors.

➤ GO LEANER

Skipping the prosciutto cuts 70 calories, 7 grams of fat and at least 485 milligrams of sodium per serving.

DIRECTIONS

Preheat the oven to 350°. Butterfly each breast by holding the knife parallel to the cutting board and slicing through the breast horizontally, starting from the thickest side, until it is almost cut in half. Leave about ¼ inch uncut on the opposite side to hold the top and bottom slices together. Open to lay flat. To make the butterflied breasts thin enough to roll, cover with plastic wrap and pound with a meat mallet. Remove plastic and season the cut side with salt and pepper.

Sprinkle 3 tablespoons of flour on a plate and place next to your work surface. On each butterflied breast, place 1 half-slice Swiss cheese, 1 slice prosciutto and ¼ of the spinach leaves and roll up the chicken over the filling. Lightly coat the roll in the flour and secure with toothpicks.

Heat the oil in a large skillet over medium-high heat. Cook the chicken rolls in the skillet, turning until lightly browned, about 5 to 8 minutes. Tongs work best for this task. Transfer the rolls to a baking dish coated with vegetable oil spray. Bake until the chicken reaches an internal temperature of 170°, about 10 to 15 minutes.

Whisk together the half-and-half, chicken broth and remaining flour in a small bowl. Pour the mixture into the same skillet and cook over medium heat, stirring until the sauce thickens, about 3 minutes. Season with salt and pepper. Place the rolls on individual serving plates, remove the toothpicks and spoon the broth mixture over each.

···

Per serving 284 calories, 10 grams total fat, 3 grams saturated fat, 5 grams monounsaturated fat, 1 gram polyunsaturated fat, 97 milligrams cholesterol, 7 grams carbohydrates, 0 grams fiber, 40 grams protein, 910 milligrams sodium

SLOW-COOKIN' CHICKEN CHILI

FROM KATHY HOLLERAN OF NEW YORK, USA

THROW THIS CHILI TOGETHER IN THE MORNING AND IT'LL BE READY TO EAT WHEN YOU GET HOME IN THE EVENING.

MAKES 5 SERVINGS | TOTAL PREP/COOK TIME: 20 MINUTES PLUS 5-6 HOURS IN SLOW COOKER

★★☆

→ FABULOUS FIBER

Thanks to all of the delicious beans, each serving of this recipe has 11 grams of fiber, which makes you feel full. When increasing fiber, increase your water intake, too.

→ DRESS IT UP

Garnish with reduced-fat shredded cheese and a dash of hot pepper sauce for spice.

INGREDIENTS

· 1 tablespoon olive oil
· 1 medium onion, peeled, diced (about 1 cup)
· 1 medium garlic clove, peeled, minced (about 1 teaspoon)
· 1 teaspoon ground cumin
· 2 (4- to 6-ounce) boneless, skinless chicken breasts, cut into 1-inch pieces
· 1 (15.5-ounce) can cannellini beans, drained, rinsed
· 1 (15.5-ounce) can chickpeas, drained, rinsed
· 1 (14-ounce) can white corn, drained, rinsed
· 2 (4-ounce) cans mild, chopped green chiles, drained
· 2 cups homemade or prepared low-sodium chicken broth
· Coarse salt and freshly ground pepper

DIRECTIONS

Heat the olive oil in a skillet over medium-high heat. Cook the onion, garlic and cumin until the onion is soft, about 5 minutes. Transfer to a slow cooker and add the chicken, beans, corn and chiles. Pour in the broth. Season with salt and pepper. Cook on high for 5 to 6 hours. Serve in bowls and garnish as desired.

. . . .

Per serving 393 calories, 6 grams total fat, 1 gram saturated fat, 5 grams monounsaturated fat, 3 grams, polyunsaturated fat, 26 milligrams cholesterol, 61 grams carbohydrates, 11 grams fiber, 27 grams protein, 454 milligrams sodium

KRISTIN'S STORY
WITH THIS DISH, I THEE WED

When my husband and I got married, I wanted to incorporate something we both loved into our special day. Chicken Vermont—a rich dish known throughout our county—was the perfect choice, but as a registered dietitian, I wanted to make it healthier. After weeks of taste-testing (yum!), I got the recipe just right and served the dish to our wedding guests. It's been a big hit anytime we've made it for friends and family since.

Easy swaps. You can often make a dish healthier without affecting flavor or texture by changing just a few ingredients. There isn't much takeout food in our area, so my husband and I make our own pizza using half whole-wheat flour and half regular flour and reduced-fat mozzarella. Or we do a taco pizza with a thin base of vegetarian refried beans, Greek yogurt in place of sour cream, reduced-fat cheddar and salsa. Instead of ground beef, we mix ground turkey with low-sodium taco seasoning.

Energy food. Before I meet my friends for Zumba class, I fuel up with a snack that has some protein and carbs. A cup of Greek yogurt and a piece of fruit, a few whole-wheat crackers and a mozzarella cheese stick or apple slices with peanut butter give me energy that lasts.

CHICKEN VERMONT

FROM KRISTIN IRACE OF VERMONT, USA

THIS ENTRÉE GETS ITS FLAVOR FROM LOCAL VERMONT FAVORITES—CHEDDAR CHEESE AND MAPLE SYRUP.

MAKES 4 SERVINGS | TOTAL PREP/COOK TIME: 30 MINUTES

★★☆

INGREDIENTS

· 4 (4- to 6-ounce) boneless, skinless chicken breasts
· ½ cup whole-wheat flour
· Coarse salt and freshly ground pepper
· 1 medium Granny Smith apple, peeled, cored, diced (about 1 cup)
· 3 ounces reduced-fat sharp cheddar cheese, grated (about 6 tablespoons)
· ¼ cup panko breadcrumbs
· 2 tablespoons olive oil
· ½ cup real maple syrup
· 1 cup orange juice
· ½ cup apple cider vinegar
· 2 teaspoons ground allspice
· 2 teaspoons ground cumin
· ½ teaspoon crushed red pepper flakes
· 2 tablespoons cornstarch

[Z] Substitute Cabot™ Sharp Extra Light Cheddar, which has 75% less fat than regular cheddar and only 1 gram of saturated fat per serving.

You can also search keywords "vegan sharp cheddar cheese" online to find creative recipes for making tangy cheddar-style nut cheeses.

DIRECTIONS

Place the chicken breasts between 2 pieces of plastic. Use a meat mallet or rolling pin to flatten them until they are ¼-inch thick. Place the flour in a bowl. Season with salt and pepper. Place the chicken in the flour, coating both sides. Remove the breasts to your work surface.

Combine the apple, cheese and breadcrumbs in a bowl. Place ¼ of the mixture on top of each chicken breast. Roll the chicken breast over the filling. Secure with a toothpick.

Heat the olive oil in a skillet over medium-high heat. Place the chicken seam-side down into the pan. Brown on all sides. Add the maple syrup, orange juice and vinegar to the pan. Stir in the allspice, cumin and red pepper flakes. Season with salt and pepper. Bring the sauce to a boil. Reduce the heat to medium. Cover and cook until the chicken reaches an internal temperature of 170°, about 15 to 20 minutes. Transfer the chicken to a serving plate and remove the toothpicks. Whisk the cornstarch into 1 tablespoon of cool water. Stir it into the sauce. Cook until the sauce thickens, about 1 to 2 minutes, and pour over the chicken.

➜ GO LIGHT
Pair this rich dish with light sides, such as steamed green beans and sliced apples. A ½ cup serving of each adds only 50 calories to the plate!

Per serving 452 calories, 11 grams total fat, 3.5 grams saturated fat, 4 grams monounsaturated fat, 1 gram polyunsaturated fat, 101 milligrams cholesterol, 46 grams carbohydrates, 1 gram fiber, 42 grams protein, 210 milligrams sodium

WHICH CURRY?

Curry paste is a moist blend of ground herbs and spices and is available where East Indian or Asian ingredients are sold. Curry pastes have differing degrees of heat: Green curry paste uses hot green chiles. Red curry paste includes red chile peppers (fresh or dried), shallots, garlic and herbs. Yellow curry paste is made with turmeric and is typically mild. Experiment by adding a small amount of curry paste to the dish and then more to taste. NOTE: Curry paste can add a lot of sodium to a dish. Look for low-sodium brands in natural-foods markets.

CHICKEN SAAG ALOO CURRY

FROM HELEN TAYLOR OF LAS PALMAS, SPAIN

CURRY PASTE DETERMINES THE FLAVOR AND THE HEAT OF THIS DISH. EXPERIMENT WITH DIFFERENT KINDS TO DISCOVER WHAT WORKS BEST FOR YOU.

MAKES 4 SERVINGS | TOTAL PREP/COOK TIME: 55 MINUTES

★★☆

INGREDIENTS
· 1 tablespoon olive oil
· 4 (4- to 6-ounce) boneless, skinless chicken breasts, cut into ½-inch pieces
· 1 large russet potato, peeled, cut into ½-inch cubes (about 1½ cups)
· 1 large yellow onion, peeled, finely diced (about 1½ cups)
· 1 large red bell pepper, seeded, deveined, cut into ½-inch pieces (about 1 cup)
· 1 large green bell pepper, seeded, deveined, cut into ½-inch pieces (about 1 cup)
· 1 fresh red chile, seeds removed and finely diced (about 1 tablespoon)
· 1-inch piece fresh ginger, peeled, grated (about 1 tablespoon)
· 4 medium garlic cloves, peeled, minced (about 1⅓ tablespoons)
· 1 (14.5-ounce) can low-sodium diced tomatoes
· 1 (10-ounce) package frozen chopped spinach, thawed
· 1 cup homemade or prepared low-sodium chicken broth
· 3 tablespoons curry paste

➔ **HEALTH BONUS**
This dish is rich in vitamins A and C!

DIRECTIONS
Heat the olive oil in a skillet over medium-high heat. Brown the chicken in the skillet, turning once. Add the potato, onion, peppers, ginger and garlic to the pan. Cook for 5 minutes. Stir in the tomatoes and chopped spinach. Pour in the broth. Stir in the curry paste. Bring the curry to a boil. Reduce the heat to medium low and cook until the potatoes are soft and the chicken is cooked through, about 20 to 30 minutes.

Per serving 445 calories, 12 grams total fat, 1 gram saturated fat, 5 grams monounsaturated fat, 1 gram polyunsaturated fat, 102 milligrams cholesterol, 38 grams carbohydrates, 8 grams fiber, 48 grams protein, 465 milligrams sodium

WALKIN' WRAP

FROM TINA NOACK OF MISSOURI, USA

MAKE IT FAST AND TAKE IT WITH YOU IN THE MORNING. YOU CAN ADD ONIONS AND PEPPERS OR OTHER FAVORITE VEGGIES, TOO.

MAKES 1 SERVING | TOTAL PREP/COOK TIME: 15 MINUTES

★★☆

INGREDIENTS

· 3 ounces lean chicken sausage such as Thin 'n Trim® brand (or substitute turkey or no-cholesterol veggie sausage)
· 2 large egg whites, beaten
· 1 ounce grated, part-skim mozzarella cheese (about ¼ cup)
· 1 (8-inch-diameter) low-sodium flour tortilla such as Whole Foods® 365™ brand
· 2 tablespoons low-sodium prepared or homemade salsa

DIRECTIONS

Spray a nonstick skillet with vegetable oil spray. Cook the sausage over medium-high heat until browned, about 5 minutes. Remove the sausage from the pan. Cook the egg whites in the skillet until opaque, about 3 minutes. Sprinkle the cheese on top and let it melt. Remove the pan from the heat.

Warm the tortilla in a conventional oven using the lowest setting or in a micro-wave oven for about 20 seconds. Lay the tortilla on a plate. Layer sausage, egg whites and salsa on the tortilla. Fold in the bottom and sides of the tortilla and roll up.

....

Per serving 420 calories, 16 grams total fat, 5 grams saturated fat, 3 grams monoun-saturated fat, 1 gram polyunsaturated fat, 80 milligrams cholesterol, 36 grams carbohy-drates, 2 grams fiber, 19 grams protein, 779 milligrams sodium

➜ MEATLESS OPTION

Go for a huevos rancheros-style wrap by skipping the chicken sausage.

JALAPEÑO CHICKEN

FROM JANELLE WALDRAM OF WASHINGTON, USA

THIS ONE'S FOR SPICY FOOD LOVERS!

MAKES 4 SERVINGS | TOTAL PREP/COOK TIME: 30 MINUTES

★★★

INGREDIENTS

· ¼ cup olive oil
· 1 teaspoon garlic powder
· 1 teaspoon lemon pepper seasoning
· ½ cup sliced marinated jalapeño peppers from a jar or can, drained
· 2 boneless, skinless chicken breasts, cut into 1-inch-long strips
· 1 large red bell pepper, seeded, deveined, cut into strips (about 1 cup)
· ½ medium white onion, peeled, chopped (about ½ cup)

DIRECTIONS

Heat the olive oil in a skillet over medium heat. Add the garlic powder, lemon pepper seasoning and the jalapeño peppers. Cook for 2 to 3 minutes. Place the chicken strips into the pan. Cook for 6 to 8 minutes on one side. Add the bell pepper and onion. Turn the chicken and cook for 5 to 8 minutes more.

....

Per serving 216 calories, 15 grams total fat, 2 grams saturated fat, 12 grams monounsaturated fat, 1 gram polyunsaturated fat, 34 milligrams cholesterol, 5 grams carbohydrates, 1 gram fiber, 14 grams protein, 365 milligrams sodium

➜ GO HOTTER

Marinated jalapeño peppers come in a can or a jar and are typically found in the international aisle of grocery stores. To kick up the fiery flavor, add a little juice from the can to the pan.

CHICKEN FETA BURGERS

FROM KATE SPEER OF PENNSYLVANIA, USA

A YUMMY ALTERNATIVE TO THE TRADITIONAL CHEESEBURGER, THIS VERSION IS MADE FROM GROUND CHICKEN AND HAS THE CHEESE MIXED RIGHT IN!
MAKES 4 SERVINGS | TOTAL PREP/COOK TIME: 15 MINUTES
★ ★ ★

INGREDIENTS
· 1 pound ground chicken (white and dark meat)
· 4 ounces feta cheese, crumbled (about ½ cup)
· ½ teaspoon ground oregano
· ½ teaspoon ground thyme
· ½ teaspoon garlic powder
· 4 marinated, roasted red pepper halves from a jar
· 4 whole-grain hamburger buns
· Lettuce (optional)
· Tomato slices (optional)

DIRECTIONS
Mix together the ground chicken, feta cheese, oregano, thyme and garlic powder in a bowl. Form into 4 patties.

Heat a grill pan or skillet over medium-high heat. Coat lightly with vegetable oil spray. Cook the burgers, turning once until no longer pink in the center, about 8 to 10 minutes. Remove the burgers to a platter. Place the roasted red peppers in the pan. Cook for 1 minute.

Place the burgers on the buns. Top with red peppers and, if desired, lettuce and tomatoes.

....

Per serving 240 calories, 9 grams total fat, 4 grams saturated fat, 3 grams monounsaturated fat, 1 gram polyunsaturated fat, 65 milligrams cholesterol, 21 grams carbohydrates, 2 grams fiber, 20 grams protein, 470 milligrams sodium

➜ **GREEK FLAIR**
Using a dab of light tzatziki sauce as a condiment adds an authentic Mediterranean touch.

"Even my picky toddler enjoys this quick and easy dish!" —KATE

NORI VEGGIE ROLLS

FROM DEBORAH MANDZUK OF ALBERTA, CANADA

LIKE SUSHI ROLLS, THIS VEGGIE VERSION IS LIGHT AND FRESH. FIND NORI IN ASIAN MARKETS AND MOST GROCERIES.

MAKES 2 SERVINGS | TOTAL PREP TIME: 20 MINUTES **V**
★ ★ ★

INGREDIENTS

· 4 sheets dried nori
· ¾ cup prepared hummus
· 1 pound fresh spinach leaves (about 4 cups)
· 2 medium carrots, peeled, trimmed, cut into matchsticks
  (about 1 cup)
· 1 large cucumber, peeled, seeded, cut into matchsticks (about 1 cup)
· 1 medium ripe tomato (or 2 Roma tomatoes), diced (about 1 cup)
· ½ large red bell pepper, seeded, deveined, cut into matchsticks
  (about ½ cup)

DIRECTIONS

Spread 3 tablespoons of hummus on 1 sheet of dried nori. Place ¼ of the spinach leaves over the hummus. Place ¼ of the remaining vegetables onto one edge of the nori sheet. Roll up the nori sheet over the veggies. *(See nori package directions for tips on rolling.)* Seal the edges by brushing with water.

Repeat with the remaining ingredients to create 4 rolls. Slice each roll diagonally into 5 or 6 pieces.

....

Per serving 232 calories, 10 grams total fat, 0 grams saturated fat, 0 grams monounsaturated fat, 0 grams polyunsaturated fat, 0 milligrams cholesterol, 30 grams carbohydrates, 11 grams fiber, 11 grams protein, 435 milligrams sodium

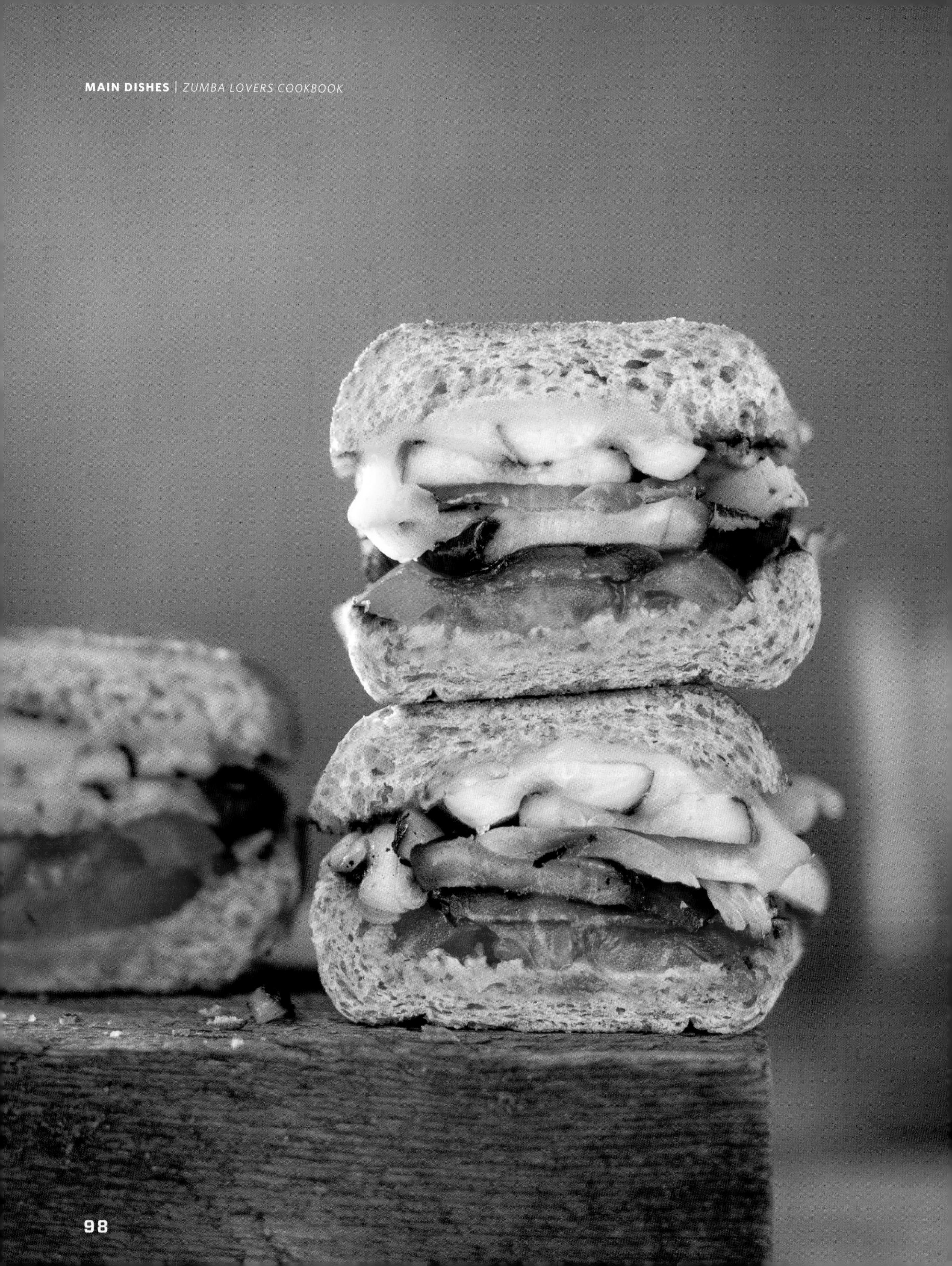

GRILLED VEGETABLE ITALIAN HOAGIE

FROM SHANNON SIMMONS OF CALIFORNIA, USA

VEGETABLES ARE THE STAR IN THIS SIMPLE, YET UPSCALE, PANINI-INSPIRED HOAGIE.

MAKES 4 SERVINGS | TOTAL PREP/COOK TIME: 1 HOUR, 20 MINUTES INCLUDING TIME TO ROAST GARLIC **V**

★★☆

INGREDIENTS
· 2 large garlic bulbs
· 3 tablespoons olive oil, divided
· Coarse salt and freshly ground pepper
· 1 (1-pound) eggplant, sliced into ¼-inch rounds
· 1 large onion, peeled, sliced into ¼-inch rounds
· 1 large zucchini, sliced lengthwise into ¼-inch strips
· 1 (12-inch-long) whole-grain hoagie roll
· 1 large tomato, cut into ¼-inch rounds
· 4 (1-ounce) slices reduced-fat pepper jack cheese, such as Cabot™ Pepper Jack Light 50% less-fat cheese

[Z] Substitute a nondairy cheddar that has low saturated fat, such as Daiya™ Pepper Jack cheese shreds.

DIRECTIONS
Preheat the oven to 350°. Cut the top fourth from the garlic bulbs to expose the cloves. Discard the tops. Season the cut side of the bulbs with 1 tablespoon olive oil, salt and pepper. Wrap the bulbs in foil, leaving a small opening at the top. Place the garlic bulb package onto a baking dish. Roast until the cloves are soft and begin to pop out of their covering, about 1 hour. Cool to room temperature. Squeeze the roasted garlic from the bulb. Mash with a fork and set aside.

Coat a grill pan with vegetable oil spray and heat pan on medium high. Brush the eggplant, onion and zucchini with 1 tablespoon olive oil and season with salt and pepper. Grill the vegetables in batches, turning once, until crisp-tender, about 3 to 4 minutes per batch.

Cut the hoagie roll in half horizontally. Place cut side down into the grill pan to toast. Remove the bread from the pan. Spread the cut side of both halves with roasted garlic. Place 1 roll half onto your work surface, garlic side up. Lay tomato slices on top of the garlic. Top with grilled vegetables. Top the veggies with cheese. Place the remaining roll half, roasted garlic side down, onto the sandwich.

Brush the outside of the sandwich with the remaining 1 tablespoon olive oil. Grill the sandwich using a panini press. Alternatively, you can place the sandwich in a nonstick skillet over medium-high heat and place another, smaller skillet on top to weigh down the sandwich. Turn when the bread begins to brown.

Cook until the sandwich is golden, the veggies are warmed through and the cheese is melting, about 4 to 5 minutes per side. Cut the sandwich into 4 pieces.

....

Per serving 291 calories, 16.5 grams total fat, 6 grams saturated fat, 9 grams monounsaturated fat, 2.5 grams polyunsaturated fat, 21 milligrams cholesterol, 38 grams carbohydrates, 7 grams fiber, 12 grams protein, 310 milligrams sodium

CHANNA MASALA (CHICKPEA CURRY)

FROM NAUSHEEN KASMANI OF WASHINGTON, USA

THIS INDIAN CURRY IS EASY TO PREPARE, AND ITS SPICES GROW MORE FRAGRANT AND FLAVORFUL THE LONGER THEY SIMMER.

MAKES 4 SERVINGS | TOTAL PREP/COOK TIME: 30 MINUTES **V**
★★★

INGREDIENTS

· 2 tablespoons olive oil
· 1 medium onion, peeled, diced (about 1 cup)
· 2 medium garlic cloves, peeled, minced (about 2 teaspoons)
· ½-inch piece fresh ginger, peeled, grated (about 1 teaspoon)
· 1 tablespoon ground cumin
· 1 teaspoon chili powder
· ½ teaspoon ground turmeric
· ½ medium lime, juiced (about 2 teaspoons)
· ½ teaspoon garam masala
· 1 (15-ounce) can diced tomatoes
· 1 (15-ounce) can chickpeas, drained, rinsed
· ½ teaspoon coarse salt

DIRECTIONS

Heat the oil in a large skillet over medium-high heat. Add the onion, garlic and ginger. Cook until soft, about 3 to 5 minutes. Reduce the heat to medium low. Sprinkle in the cumin, chili powder, turmeric and garam masala. Cook for 2 minutes more. Stir in the tomatoes and simmer, scraping up any bits that have stuck to the pan. Add ⅓ cup water and the chickpeas. Simmer uncovered for 5 to 8 minutes. Season with salt and lime juice.

....

Per serving 218 calories, 9 grams total fat, 1 gram saturated fat, 6 grams monounsaturated fat, 1 gram polyunsaturated fat, 0 milligrams cholesterol, 31 grams carbohydrates, 6 grams fiber, 6 grams protein, 352 milligrams sodium

➜ **make it a meal**
Serve with Indian flatbread and brown or basmati rice.

PAPADUM

A thin, crisp, cracker-like bread, papadum (also known as papad) is eaten with Indian chutneys and curries. Look for packages of un-cooked papadum in markets that sell Indian specialty foods and follow the package directions for preparation.

One popular method for cooking papadum is to heat it directly over an open flame on a gas stove *(see following pages).* For your safety, use long tongs that allow you to hold the bread at a distance. Heat over a medium flame until the edges are slightly brown. Let the papadum cool. Break off pieces to scoop up channa masala and other favorite curry dishes.

VEGGIE & RICE STUFFED BELL PEPPERS

FROM CHARISE RICHARDS OF TEXAS, USA

➜ **Give it an A+**

Thanks to all of the colorful peppers in this recipe, each serving provides 720% of the recommended daily intake for vitamin A—a key player in a healthy immune system.

[Z] For a dish with little to no saturated fat, try a cheddar-style soy cheese that's made for melting, such as Teese.

THIS DISH DELIGHTS THE SENSES! UP THE HEAT BY SUBBING POBLANOS FOR THE ORANGE BELL PEPPERS.

MAKES 6 SERVINGS | *TOTAL PREP/COOK TIME: 45 MINUTES* **V**
★ ★ ☆

INGREDIENTS

· 2 tablespoons olive oil, divided
· 1 pint fresh mushrooms, sliced (about 1 cup)
· 1 large green bell pepper, seeded, deveined, chopped (about 1 cup)
· 1 large yellow bell pepper, seeded, deveined, chopped (about 1 cup)
· 1 red onion, peeled, diced (about 1 cup)
· 1 (14.5-ounce) can corn, drained
· 1 (14.5-ounce) can diced tomatoes (or substitute fire-roasted diced tomatoes)
· Coarse salt and freshly ground pepper
· 1 cup uncooked jasmine rice (expands to 2 cups cooked)
· ½ cup chopped fresh cilantro
· Zest of 3 medium limes (about 1½ tablespoons)
· 3 medium limes, juiced (about 5-6 tablespoons)
· 6 large orange bell peppers, selected to stand
· 4 ounces reduced-fat cheddar cheese, grated (about 1 cup)

DIRECTIONS

Preheat the oven to 350°. Heat 1 tablespoon olive oil in a skillet over medium-high heat. Add the mushrooms, green and yellow peppers, and onion. Add the corn and tomatoes. Season with salt and pepper. Cook until the vegetables are soft, about 5 minutes.

Prepare the rice according to the directions on the package. Place the cooked rice into a bowl. Toss with cilantro, lime zest and lime juice.

Cut off and reserve the top of each orange bell pepper. Scoop out the veins and seeds and discard them. Place peppers open side up into a baking dish coated with vegetable oil spray. Place half of the vegetables into the bottom of the peppers. Add a layer of cheese. Spoon the rice over the cheese and then top with the remaining vegetables. Drizzle with the remaining 1 tablespoon olive oil. Place the tops back onto the peppers. Bake until the peppers are soft, about 20 minutes.

··

Per serving 350 calories, 11 grams total fat, 5 grams saturated fat, 4 grams monounsaturated fat, 1 gram polyunsaturated fat, 4 milligrams cholesterol, 53 grams carbohydrates, 9 grams fiber, 13 grams protein, 310 milligrams sodium

CHARISE'S STORY
SURVIVING & THRIVING

Fit at 48, I was the last person anyone expected to be diagnosed with Stage IV colorectal cancer. And if you'd told me that a year after chemo and 32 rounds of radiation I'd be teaching Zumba classes, I'd have called you crazy. But here I am—happy to be alive and dancing four days a week!

Food for life. Like many survivors, I need to eat differently now. I can't have food or water before class because of the way they affect my system, so I have a protein drink right after cooldown to replenish energy and vitamins. Before cancer I wouldn't have thought twice about going out for fried tacos and margaritas—thinking I could "dance off" the fat and calories in the gym. Now I have alcohol and fried food a few times a year and make dancing its own reward.

Since I can no longer handle raw food, I flash-cook veggies in a wok with a little oil. Very lean meats are paired with fresh, vibrant sides, like a bright orange baked sweet potato and steamed broccoli. My go-to lunch is cooked egg whites, tomato and fat-free cheese in a flaxseed pita—a great choice of bread with omega-3s, no trans fats and few carbs.

Making it count. Cancer taught me that some things are beyond my control, but a chance to keep living my life is worth a few diet changes. Now I make every bite—and every moment—matter!

LOSING THE BABY WEIGHT

After having my second baby, my husband started calling me "Big Mama"—not just because I'm a great mom but because I weighed more than he did! And for some reason, the diet I'd been following most of my life didn't work anymore.

Before my pregnancies, all I needed to do to lose weight was cut back on sugar, carbs and milk for two weeks. Now, this only caused me to eat more of everything else. My hormones and cravings were out of control, and I was hungry *all* the time.

Better-quality fuel. After doing some nutrition research, I learned to check food labels, manage portions, get more raw food into my diet and adopt new ways to replace refined sugar. I now enjoy almond or rice milk in place of some dairy and often broil a nice piece of fish instead of having meat every day.

I also learned that iron plays a very important role for my children and me, especially now that I'm dancing so much in Zumba classes. For good sources of energy, I've added beans, lentils and split peas to most of my meals.

Better results. Thanks to the greater variety of ingredients I now use to feed my family, my diet has changed for the better. My weight is under control, and I'm healthier for it!

LETTUCE-WRAP TACOS
FROM ALYTA MEJIA-KIVISELS OF TEXAS, USA

WHEN YOU'RE CRAVING TACOS, THIS LIGHT, NO-TORTILLA VERSION REALLY SATISFIES.
MAKES 4 SERVINGS | TOTAL PREP/COOK TIME: 30 MINUTES
★★☆

INGREDIENTS
· 1 tablespoon olive oil
· 1 small red onion, peeled, finely diced (about ½ cup)
· 2 medium garlic cloves, peeled, minced (about 2 teaspoons)
· 1 pound lean ground beef (or substitute diced fish or ground chicken)
· Coarse salt and freshly ground pepper
· 1 (15.5-ounce) can refried beans
· 1 cup cooked brown rice
· 1 medium ripe avocado, seed removed, peeled, diced (about 1 cup)
· 1 medium ripe tomato, diced (about 1 cup)
· Leafy lettuce (such as Romaine or bibb)
· Fresh salsa (optional)
· Lime wedges (optional)
· Chopped fresh cilantro (optional)

➔ VEGGIE VERSION
Swap the beef and beans for vegetarian refried beans, found in most groceries. Try adding finely chopped green peppers, carrots and mushrooms.

DIRECTIONS
Heat the olive oil in a skillet over medium-high heat. Add the onions and garlic and cook until soft, about 4 to 5 minutes. Add the ground beef and cook, breaking up large clumps, until browned, about 5 minutes more. Season with salt and pepper. Place the beef into a serving bowl.

Warm the refried beans in a pan over medium-high heat. Scoop into a serving bowl. Place the rice, avocado and tomato into separate bowls.

Remove and rinse 4 of the largest outer leaves from the head of lettuce and pat dry. Place each leaf of lettuce onto a separate plate and fill leaves with beef, beans, rice, avocado and tomato. Roll up each lettuce leaf burrito-style. Garnish, if desired, with salsa, lime wedges and cilantro.

....

Per serving 410 calories, 18 grams total fat, 4.5 grams saturated fat, 9 grams monounsaturated fat, 2 grams polyunsaturated fat, 70 milligrams cholesterol, 33 grams carbohydrates, 11 grams fiber, 33 grams protein, 230 milligrams sodium

FAST 'N' FRESH FISH TACOS

EUGENIA ROMERO OF OHIO, USA

IT'S A FOOD FIESTA! MAKE THESE COLORFUL TACOS WITH TILAPIA OR THE FRESHEST FISH YOU CAN FIND.

MAKES 6 SERVINGS | TOTAL PREP/COOK TIME: 30 MINUTES

★ ★ ★

INGREDIENTS

· ½ medium ripe avocado, seed removed, peeled, diced (about ½ cup)
· ⅓ cup plain low-fat yogurt
· 1 large lime, juiced (about 2 tablespoons)
· Zest of 1 medium lime (about 1-2 teaspoons)
· ½ teaspoon chili powder
· Coarse salt and freshly ground pepper
· 3 (6-ounce) tilapia fillets
· 1 teaspoon garlic powder
· 1 teaspoon paprika
· 1 tablespoon olive oil
· 6 (6-inch) corn tortillas
· ½ medium head romaine lettuce, thinly sliced (about 3 cups)
· ½ small red cabbage, shredded (about 2 cups)
· 2 large cucumbers, peeled, seeded, diced into ½-inch pieces (about 2 cups)
· 1 bunch radishes, thinly sliced (about 1 cup)
· Chopped cilantro (optional)

➜ GO SPICY

If you like cumin, add some to the fish seasoning before cooking.

DIRECTIONS

Place the avocado, yogurt, lime juice, lime zest and chili powder into the bowl of a food processor. Pulse until smooth. Season with salt and pepper. Transfer to a bowl and set aside.

Season the fish with the garlic powder, paprika and salt and pepper. Heat the olive oil in a skillet over medium heat. Cook the fish, turning once, until opaque, about 3 minutes per side. Transfer to a platter and use a fork to gently break apart the fish into bite-size pieces.

Warm the tortillas in a microwave oven for up to 20 seconds or in an oven on the lowest setting. To assemble, place one tortilla on a plate. Top with ⅙ of the fish, ⅙ of the veggies and ⅙ of the sauce. Repeat with the remaining tortillas and filling. Garnish with cilantro if desired.

. . . .

Per serving 195 calories, 6 grams total fat, 1 gram saturated fat, 3 grams monounsaturated fat, 1 gram polyunsaturated fat, 41 milligrams cholesterol, 18 grams carbohydrates, 4 grams fiber, 19.5 grams protein, 103 milligrams sodium

EUGENIA'S STORY
TEACHABLE MOMENTS

Last year I weighed 267 pounds. I wanted to teach my 4-year-old daughter the importance of being active and eating healthier but never thought I would find a physical activity that I could stick to myself.

Inspired to change. Then I met my very supportive Zumba family and wanted to go to class all the time! My daughter became a fan, too, and every Friday night, we'd do Zumba moves together. That motivated me to change my eating habits, and now I'm getting more vegetables, fruits, whole grains and lean meats in my diet, while reducing processed foods. I'm also watching my portions, cooking more often and trying new recipes to get more variety into our diet.

Setting an example. All this is showing my daughter that eating right is not about depriving yourself of food but about choosing the best foods to keep you healthy. So far I've lost 60 pounds, and my goal is to lose a total of 100. Although I do hit the occasional plateau, I know I'll make it, because I'm committed to these habits as a new way of life.

TILAPIA À LA KAUACHI

FROM LIZ GANNON OF ILLINOIS, USA

NAMED FOR THE AUTHOR'S MEXICAN-AMERICAN FAMILY, THIS SPICY FISH DISH MAKES GREAT USE OF STAPLES IN THEIR EVERYDAY DIET.

MAKES 4 SERVINGS | TOTAL PREP/COOK TIME: 40 MINUTES

★★☆

INGREDIENTS

· 4 tablespoons olive oil, divided
· 2 large limes, juiced (about 3-4 tablespoons), divided
· 1 teaspoon liquid smoke flavoring (*see page 45 for information on liquid smoke*)
· 2 (8-ounce) tilapia fillets, cut into 4 pieces (or substitute catfish or snapper)
· Coarse salt and freshly ground pepper
· ½ medium white onion, peeled, sliced (about ½ cup)
· 2 medium garlic cloves, peeled, minced (about 2 teaspoons)
· 4 medium Roma tomatoes, chopped (about 2 cups)
· 2 serrano peppers, seeded, deveined, diced (about 2 tablespoons)
· 3 tablespoons chopped fresh cilantro leaves

DIRECTIONS

Whisk together 2 tablespoons olive oil, the juice of 1 lime and liquid smoke flavoring. Coat both sides of the fish with the seasoned oil. Season with salt and pepper.

Heat the remaining 2 tablespoons olive oil in a large skillet over medium-low heat. Cook the onion in the pan until transparent, about 4 to 5 minutes. Add the garlic, tomatoes and peppers. Continue to cook until the tomatoes release most of their water and begin to brown slightly. Push vegetables to the outside of the pan. Place the fillets into the center and spoon the vegetables over top. Cover the pan with a lid and cook for 5 minutes more. Remove the lid. Add the cilantro and sprinkle with the remaining lime juice. Cook on medium-high heat until the meatiest part of the fish is firm, about 5 more minutes.

....

Per serving 233 calories, 13 grams total fat, 2 grams saturated fat, 8 grams monounsaturated fat, 2 grams polyunsaturated fat, 57 milligrams cholesterol, 8 grams carbohydrates, 2 grams fiber, 21 grams protein, 74 milligrams sodium

→ **BRING THE HEAT**

A serrano pepper has more bite and heat than its cousin the jalapeño. If you're a true spice fan, feel free to add more.

WHOLE RED SNAPPER WITH ROSEMARY

FROM ALEJANDRA BURRONE OF NORTH CAROLINA, USA

SNAPPER IS A DELICIOUS AND DELICATE WHITE, FLAKY FISH. IF YOU CAN'T FIND IT AT YOUR LOCAL FISHMONGER, ASK FOR THE FRESHEST SUBSTITUTE.

MAKES 4 SERVINGS | TOTAL PREP/COOK TIME: 1 HOUR
★★★

INGREDIENTS

· 1 (3- to 3½-pound) fresh whole red snapper, cleaned with
  scales removed (yields about 4 6-ounce fillets)
· 2 tablespoons olive oil
· Coarse salt and freshly ground pepper
· 1 medium lemon, juiced (about 3 tablespoons)
· 1 fennel bulb, tops trimmed, cored, thinly sliced (about 1 cup)
· ½ medium white onion, peeled, chopped (about ½ cup)
· 6 sprigs fresh rosemary
· 2 medium garlic cloves, peeled, sliced (about 2 teaspoons)
· Lemon slices for garnish

DIRECTIONS

Preheat the oven to 400°. Coat a roasting pan with vegetable oil spray. Brush the fish inside and out with olive oil. Season the skin and the cavity with salt and pepper. Drizzle lemon juice over and inside. Place the fennel, onion, rosemary and garlic into the cavity of the fish. Bake uncovered until the fish is flaky, about 40 minutes.

To serve, carefully pull back the skin. Use a very sharp knife to separate the flesh from the backbone. Cut the top fillet into 2 portions. Discard the herbs and vegetables. Lift the fish backbone and head from the bottom fillet. Cut the bottom fillet into 2 portions. Garnish with lemon slices.

. . . .

Per serving 267 calories, 10 grams total fat, 2 grams saturated fat, 5 grams monounsaturated fat, 1 gram polyunsaturated fat, 63 milligrams cholesterol, 8 grams carbohydrates, 3 grams fiber, 36 grams protein, 124 milligrams sodium

"I like this dish because it's healthy, easy to prepare and low-calorie." —ALEJANDRA

CEVICHE WITH SWEET POTATOES & YUCA

FROM VANESSA MILLS OF FLORIDA, USA

HERE'S A TWIST ON A TRADITIONAL SOUTH AND CENTRAL AMERICAN DISH. SERVE IT AS A MAIN COURSE OR A TASTY APPETIZER.

MAKES 2 SERVINGS | TOTAL PREP/COOK TIME: 1 HOUR, 5 MINUTES INCLUDING TIME TO MARINATE 🌶

★★★

INGREDIENTS

· 2 large limes, juiced (about 3-4 tablespoons)
· 1 medium celery rib, sliced (about ⅓ cup)
· 1 tablespoon chopped fresh cilantro
· ½ teaspoon ground cumin
· 1 medium garlic clove, peeled, minced (about 1 teaspoon)
· 1 large jalapeño pepper, seeded, deveined, diced (about 2 tablespoons)
· Coarse salt and freshly ground pepper
· 4 ounces fresh tilapia cut into ½-inch cubes
· 1 small sweet potato, peeled, diced (about 1½ cups)
· 1 small yuca root, peeled, diced (about 1-1½ cups)
· 1 medium red onion, peeled, thinly sliced (about 1 cup)
· Bibb lettuce, separated into whole leaves (or substitute with Boston lettuce)

DIRECTIONS

Place the lime juice, celery, cilantro and cumin into the bowl of a blender. Purée until smooth. Pour into a large glass bowl. Stir in the garlic and jalapeño pepper and season with salt and pepper. Add the tilapia and gently stir until coated. Let it marinate until the fish is opaque and firm to the touch, about 1 hour.

While the fish is marinating, place the sweet potato and yuca root in a pot and cover with water. Bring to a boil over medium-high heat. Reduce the heat to medium low and cook until both are easily pierced with a fork, about 20 minutes.

Place the onion slices in a bowl of warm water and let stand 10 minutes. Drain and set aside.

To serve, add the sweet potato and yuca root to the ceviche. Add the onions. Toss to combine. For a beautiful presentation, use the whole lettuce leaves as bowls to hold the ceviche.

....

Per serving 185 calories, 1 gram total fat, 0 grams saturated fat, 0 grams monounsaturated fat, 0 grams polyunsaturated fat, 17.5 milligrams cholesterol, 36 grams carbohydrates, 3.5 grams fiber, 9 grams protein, 65 milligrams sodium

➜ FIRE IT UP!

If you can handle the heat, try a more intense habañero pepper in place of the jalapeño. But beware! Never touch your eyes while working with chile peppers and always wash your hands thoroughly after handling them.

ABOUT YUCA ROOT

Yuca *(YOO-cuh)* is a Latin root vegetable becoming available in grocery stores everywhere. Not to be confused with the yucca *(YUH-cuh)* plant, which is used in herbal supplements and hair care products, the yuca root looks like a long potato, varying in color from yellow to brown. It's high in vitamins A, B and C and is a source of calcium, phosphorous, iron, manganese and copper. Its tough outer bark looks menacing but is easily removed with a sharp knife. Yuca root should be cooked well before eating. It can be toxic when eaten raw or when heated below 167°.

SHRIMP & SCALLOP CEVICHE

FROM COLLEEN GAZZALLA OF FLORIDA, USA

LIGHT, WITH A SPICY LATIN FLAIR, THIS DISH IS FUN TO SHARE WITH FRIENDS. INVITE THEM FOR A SPECIAL AFTER-CLASS MEAL.

MAKES 8 SERVINGS | TOTAL PREP/COOK TIME: 30 MINUTES PLUS 2 HOURS TO MARINATE

★ ★ ★

INGREDIENTS
· 1 pound fresh large shrimp, peeled, deveined (about 31-35)
· 1 pound bay scallops
· 4 cups fresh lime juice
· 2 medium ripe avocados, seeds removed, peeled, diced (about 2 cups)
· ½ large red onion, peeled, diced (about ½ cup)
· 2 large jalapeño peppers, seeded, deveined, finely diced (about ¼ cup)
· ¼ cup chopped fresh cilantro
· ½ teaspoon red pepper flakes (optional)
· Coarse salt
· Chopped fresh cilantro for garnish

DIRECTIONS
Bring a pot of water to a boil over medium-high heat. Add the shrimp to the pot and cook for 30 seconds. Use a slotted spoon to transfer the shrimp to a bowl filled with ice water. Use the spoon to drain and transfer the shrimp to a work surface. Repeat this procedure for the scallops.

Cut the seafood into bite-size pieces. Place shrimp and scallops in a large glass bowl. Pour 3 cups of the lime juice over the seafood. Cover and refrigerate for 1 hour.

In a bowl, mix together the avocados, onion, jalapeño peppers and cilantro. Add the red pepper flakes if using. Remove the seafood from the refrigerator and drain. Toss the avocado-and-onion mixture with the seafood. Pour in the remaining 1 cup of lime juice. Season with salt. Refrigerate for 1 hour more. Drain the ceviche before serving. Garnish with additional cilantro.

....

Per serving 207 calories, 7 grams total fat, 1 gram saturated fat, 4 grams monounsaturated fat, 1 gram polyunsaturated fat, 105 milligrams cholesterol, 17 grams carbohydrates, 2 grams fiber, 22 grams protein, 181 milligrams sodium

SALMON STEW WITH BLACK BEANS

FROM SARAH WINTERS OF OHIO, USA

GREEN TOMATOES HAVE A TANGY FLAVOR THAT COMPLEMENTS THE SPICES IN THIS STEW. FOR AN EXTRA KICK, ADD A DASH OR TWO OF CAYENNE PEPPER.

MAKES 4 SERVINGS | TOTAL PREP/COOK TIME: 30 MINUTES

★★★

INGREDIENTS

· 2 tablespoons olive oil, divided
· 2 (4- to 6-ounce) boneless, skinless salmon fillets, cut into 1-inch cubes
· 1 medium white onion, peeled, chopped (about 1 cup)
· 1 large green bell pepper, seeded, deveined, chopped (about 1 cup)
· 2 firm green tomatoes, chopped (about 1 cup)
· 1 large jalapeño pepper, seeded, deveined, diced (about 2 tablespoons)
· 2 medium garlic cloves, peeled, minced (about 2 teaspoons)
· 1½ teaspoons ground cumin
· 1½ teaspoons chili powder
· 1 large lime, juiced (about 2 tablespoons)
· Coarse salt and freshly ground pepper
· 1 (15.5-ounce) can black beans, drained, rinsed

DIRECTIONS

Heat 1 tablespoon olive oil in a skillet over medium-high heat. Add the salmon and cook, turning cubes once, until brown on top and bottom. Remove the salmon to a platter.

Add 1 tablespoon olive oil, the onions and bell pepper to the skillet. Cook until the vegetables are soft, about 2 to 3 minutes. Add the tomatoes, jalapeño peppers and garlic. Stir in the cumin, chili powder and lime juice, and season with salt and pepper. Reduce the heat to medium low. Stir in the black beans. Add the salmon back into the pan. Cover the pan with a lid and cook for 8 to 10 minutes.

....

Per serving 241 calories, 9 grams total fat, 1 gram saturated fat, 5 grams monounsaturated fat, 1 gram polyunsaturated fat, 18 milligrams cholesterol, 25 grams carbohydrates, 8 grams fiber, 15 grams protein, 233 milligrams sodium

BAKED MOROCCAN FISH TAGINE

FROM RACHEL NEWCOMB OF FLORIDA, USA

THIS RECIPE IS FILLED WITH THE HEALTHFUL INGREDIENTS OF A MEDITERRANEAN DIET.

MAKES 4 SERVINGS | TOTAL PREP/COOK TIME: 1 HOUR

★★★

INGREDIENTS

Marinade
· ½ cup chopped cilantro
· 2 medium garlic cloves, crushed
· 1 teaspoon ground cumin
· 1 teaspoon ground paprika
· ¼ teaspoon ground cayenne pepper
· 4 tablespoons olive oil
· 1 medium lemon, juiced (about 3 tablespoons)

Fish & Vegetables
· 4 (6-ounce) cod fillets (or substitute available white fish)
· Coarse salt and freshly ground pepper
· 5 medium carrots, peeled, cut into 2-inch pieces (about 2½ cups)
· 4 medium Yukon Gold potatoes, peeled, cut into ¼ inch-thick slices
· 2 tablespoons olive oil
· 3 medium tomatoes, peeled, seeded, cut into ¼ inch-thick slices
· ½ lemon, sliced

➜ SOME LIKE IT HOT!
Make this dish extra spicy by roasting three jalapeño peppers along with the potato and tomato mixture.

DIRECTIONS

Preheat the oven to 425°. Combine the marinade ingredients in a food processor or blender and pulse several times, leaving the marinade a bit chunky. Pour half of the marinade into a high-sided glass baking dish and reserve the rest for later. Season the cod fillets with salt and pepper and lay them in the marinade, coating the fish on all sides. Let marinate for 30 minutes while you prepare the vegetables.

In a bowl, toss the carrots and potato slices with the olive oil and spread the mixture in a large roasting pan coated with vegetable oil spray. Top with tomato slices and brush with reserved marinade. Sprinkle with salt and pepper. Roast for 20 minutes, turning once, or until the potatoes and carrots are almost cooked through.

Remove the fish from the marinade and place on top of the vegetable mixture in the roasting pan. Arrange lemon slices over the fish. Roast 10 to 12 minutes or until the fish flakes easily with a fork. Serve with crusty bread for dipping into the sauce.

....

Per serving 460 calories, 12 grams total fat, 1.5 grams saturated fat, 2 grams monounsaturated fat, 8 grams polyunsaturated fat, 65 milligrams cholesterol, 53 grams total carbohydrates, 10 grams fiber, 37 grams protein, 196 milligrams sodium

DESSERTS

SWEET EATS & TREATS

Boy, do Zumba lovers like chocolate! While only a few of you submitted desserts for this book, most of the recipes we received were variations on popular chocolate dishes. Here are our favorites, including Whole-Wheat Coconut Zucchini Brownies *(page 117)* and Chocolate Rum Cupcakes with Orange Rum Sauce *(page 120)*.

We love that these recipes feature some pretty wholesome ingredients—rolled oats, pecans, fresh fruit, dark chocolate. Want something light and refreshing? Try the Mixed-Berry Crisp *(page 123)* or the Fruity Summer Granita *(page 124)*. If you're watching your waist, make dishes lighter with the tips here and in the "Glossary & Substitutions" section *(page 145)*. You'll also find snacks in the "On the Go" section *(page 128)* to satisfy any sweet tooth.

....

★★★ **ZUMBA ALL-STARS**
★★☆ **OCCASIONAL EATS**
★☆☆ **SOMETIME SPLURGES**

GREAT DATES

You can make a natural, nutrient-rich sweetener from fresh dates!

➤ *What to buy.* Medjool dates are ideal—plump and sweet. Soak them in water to make it easier to remove pits by hand, or find pitted dates online or in most groceries and natural-foods markets.

➤ *Two easy steps.* Place pitted dates in a saucepan, cover with water and simmer until they're soft. Drain the water and purée the dates in a food processor or high-powered blender. If needed, add a tablespoon of water to achieve a creamy consistency.

➤ *How to store it.* Refrigerate extra paste in an airtight container. To store large quantities for up to 3 months, try this tip from Sarahfaé of www.addictedtoveggies.com: Divide date paste into freezer bags in 1-cup batches. Seal the bags and stack flat in the freezer. When needed, break off and thaw a piece—or thaw the whole bag. *For more on dates, see "Sugar & Sweeteners," page 149.*

CHOCOLATE COCONUT CHEESECAKE

FROM LIZ ROLLAND OF MARYLAND, USA

WE KNOW. WE HAD YOU AT "CHEESECAKE."

MAKES 12 SERVINGS | TOTAL PREP/COOK TIME: 1 HOUR, 25 MINUTES PLUS TIME TO REFRIGERATE OVERNIGHT Ⓥ

★☆☆

INGREDIENTS
· 1 cup old-fashioned rolled oats
· 1 cup pecan pieces
· 2 tablespoons butter
· ½ cup shredded sweetened coconut
· 6 ounces dark chocolate chips, melted
· 8 ounces reduced-fat cream cheese, softened (or substitute Neufchâtel cheese)
· ½ cup natural granulated sugar
· 3 large eggs
· 1 teaspoon pure vanilla extract
· 1 (16-ounce) container low-fat (1% milk fat) cottage cheese

[Z] Substitute 1½ tablespoons canola oil.

[Z] Substitute ¼ cup Stevia in the Raw® (or favorite no-calorie sweetener) + ¼ cup date paste (see "Great Dates," this page).

DIRECTIONS
Preheat the oven to 350°. Place the oats, nuts and butter into the bowl of a food processor and pulse until crumbs are formed. Place the crumbs into the bottom of a springform pan. To form the crust, use your fingers to press the crumbs along the bottom of the pan and up the sides until it is covered. Sprinkle the coconut over the crust. Bake until the coconut is golden and the crust is set, about 10 to 12 minutes. Cool to room temperature. Reduce the heat to 300°.

Use an electric mixer to combine the melted chocolate with the cream cheese. Stir in the sugar until creamy. Add the eggs 1 at a time. Stir in the vanilla extract. Mix in the cottage cheese until smooth. Pour the filling into the crust. Bake until the center of the cheesecake is just set, about 50 to 55 minutes. Unlatch the spring and release the cake from the pan. Allow the cheesecake to cool, then refrigerate uncovered overnight.

➤ **GO NUTS!**
Walnuts, peanuts, macadamia nuts and almonds are all tasty alternatives to the pecans in this crust.

➤ **NOT INTO COCONUT?**
Skip it and make this a chocolate cheesecake.

Per serving 310 calories, 18 grams total fat, 8 grams saturated fat, 4.5 grams monounsaturated fat, 2.5 grams polyunsaturated fat, 70 milligrams cholesterol, 27 grams carbohydrates, 2 grams fiber, 10 grams protein, 260 milligrams sodium

WHOLE-WHEAT COCONUT ZUCCHINI BROWNIES

INSPIRED BY A RECIPE FROM BATRICE ADAMS OF NEW JERSEY, USA

HERE'S A NEW APPROACH TO THE OLD-FASHIONED BROWNIE.
MAKES 18 SERVINGS | TOTAL PREP/COOK TIME: 1 HOUR **V**
★ ☆ ☆

INGREDIENTS
· 1 medium zucchini, shredded (about 1 cup)
· 1 cup extra-virgin coconut oil
· 2 medium bananas
· ½ cup date paste (see "Great Dates," page 116)
· ¾ cup Stevia in the Raw® (or substitute favorite no-calorie sweetener)
· 1 cup whole-wheat baking mix (such as Bisquick® Whole Grain Mix)
· ⅔ cup unsweetened cocoa powder
· 1 teaspoon coarse salt
· 4 large eggs
· 1 teaspoon pure vanilla extract
· ¾ cup unsweetened coconut flakes

DIRECTIONS
Preheat the oven to 325°. Place the zucchini into a colander. Press with a paper towel to drain excess moisture. Coat a jelly-roll pan (baking sheet with 1-inch lip) with vegetable oil spray.

Use an electric mixer to combine the coconut oil, bananas, date paste and stevia. In a separate bowl, whisk together the baking mix, cocoa powder and salt. Stir the dry mixture into the wet mixture. Mix in the eggs and vanilla extract. Stir in the zucchini and coconut flakes until thoroughly combined.

Pour the batter into the pan and use a spatula to spread evenly. Bake until a tester inserted into the center comes out clean, about 20 to 25 minutes. Cool on a baking rack. Cut into 18 squares.

....

Per serving 90 calories, 2.5 grams total fat, 1 gram saturated fat, .5 grams monounsaturated fat, 0 grams polyunsaturated fat, 47 milligrams cholesterol, 15 grams carbohydrates, 2.5 grams fiber, 3 grams protein, 167 milligrams sodium

PUMPKIN MOUSSE

FROM RITA ZAPIEN OF TEXAS, USA

IT'S COLD-WEATHER COMFORT FOOD—SILKY SMOOTH AND MADE WITHOUT HEAVY CREAM.
MAKES 8 SERVINGS | TOTAL PREP/COOK TIME: 2 HOURS, 20 MINUTES INCLUDING TIME TO REFRIGERATE
★ ☆ ☆

INGREDIENTS
· 1 tablespoon gelatin powder, unflavored (or substitute agar-agar powder, see page 150)
· 1 (16-ounce) container fat-free cottage cheese
· 8 ounces fat-free cream cheese, softened
· 1 (15-ounce) can pumpkin purée
· ¾ cup superfine sugar (or substitute turbinado sugar)
· 1 tablespoon pure vanilla extract
· 1 teaspoon pumpkin pie spice
· Gingersnap cookie for garnish (optional)

[Z] Substitute ¼ cup + 2 tablespoons Stevia in the Raw® (or favorite no-calorie sweetener) + ¼ cup date paste (see "Great Dates," page 116).

DIRECTIONS
Pour 3 tablespoons of water into a small saucepan and sprinkle the gelatin on top. Let stand for about 2 minutes. Stir over medium heat for 2 minutes, until the gelatin has dissolved completely. Cool to room temperature.

Purée the cottage cheese in a food processor until smooth. Add the cream cheese, pumpkin, sugar, vanilla extract and pumpkin pie spice. Pulse until smooth. Transfer to a bowl.

Fold the gelatin into the mousse. Cover and refrigerate for 2 hours. Pour into serving bowls and crumble a small piece of gingersnap on top if desired.

....

Per serving 190 calories, 0 grams total fat, 0 grams saturated fat, 0 grams monounsaturated fat, 0 grams polyunsaturated fat, 10 milligrams cholesterol, 28 grams carbohydrates, 2 grams fiber, 19 grams protein, 410 milligrams sodium

→ **Vegetarian?**
If you're avoiding animal-based gelatin, agar-agar powder is a veg-friendly option. See "Thickeners," page 150.

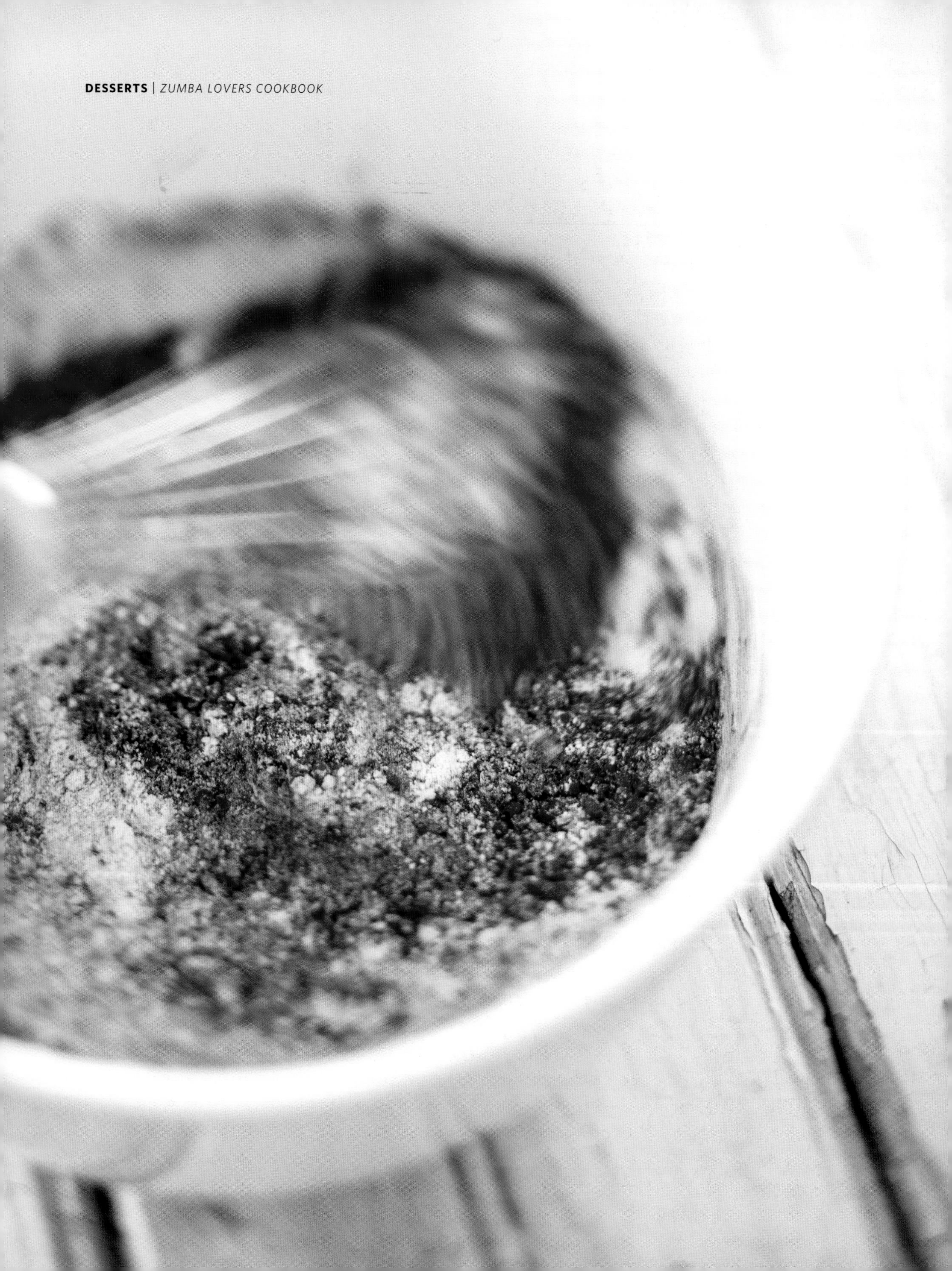

CHOCOLATE ZUCCHINI CAKE WITH CREAM CHEESE FROSTING

INSPIRED BY A RECIPE FROM JULIE CISON OF MINNESOTA, USA

WHEN YOU CRAVE CHOCOLATE, THIS REALLY SATISFIES!
MAKES 16 SERVINGS | TOTAL PREP/COOK TIME: 1 HOUR **V**
★ ☆ ☆

INGREDIENTS
Cake
· 2 cups white whole-wheat flour
· ¼ cup Stevia in the Raw® (or substitute favorite no-calorie sweetener)
· ¾ cup unsweetened baking cocoa powder
· 1 teaspoon baking powder
· 2 teaspoons baking soda
· ½ teaspoon salt
· 1 teaspoon ground cinnamon
· 4 large eggs
· ½ cup date paste (see "Great Dates," page 116)
· 1 cup unsweetened applesauce
· 3 medium zucchini, shredded (about 3 cups)
· ¾ cup chopped pecans

Frosting
· ¼ cup white whole-wheat flour
· 1 (8-ounce) package reduced-fat cream cheese, room temperature
· ½ teaspoon pure vanilla extract
· ½ cup Stevia in the Raw® (or substitute favorite no-calorie sweetener)

DIRECTIONS
Cake. Preheat the oven to 350°. Coat a 9 x 13-inch baking pan with vegetable oil spray. Whisk together the flour, stevia, baking cocoa, baking powder, baking soda, salt and cinnamon in a large bowl. In a separate bowl, whisk the eggs, date paste and applesauce together. Stir in the zucchini. Add the wet ingredients to the dry ingredients, stirring until just combined. Fold in the pecans. Pour the batter into the pan. Bake until a knife inserted into the center comes out clean, about 40 to 45 minutes. Allow the cake to cool.

Frosting. Place the flour and ½ cup water into a saucepan and cook over medium-low heat until a pudding consistency is achieved. Use an electric mixer to combine the cream cheese with the flour mixture. Stir in the vanilla extract and stevia. Spread over the top of the cake.

....

Per serving 185 calories, 8 grams total fat, 2 grams saturated fat, 3 grams monounsaturated fat, 1.5 grams polyunsaturated fat, 60 milligrams cholesterol, 24 grams carbohydrates, 4 grams fiber, 7 grams protein, 316 milligrams sodium

Stevia 411

Stevia in the Raw® is sold in small packets and in a baker's bag for use in larger quantities. It's formulated to substitute for table sugar in equal amounts. Other brands of liquid and powdered stevia range dramatically in their levels of sweetness—up to 300 times as sweet as table sugar—so follow package directions or check the product's website for conversion advice. *For more on stevia, see "Sugar & Substitutes," page 149.*

CHOCOLATE RUM CUPCAKES WITH ORANGE RUM SAUCE

FROM TOSHA LEE OF TEXAS, USA

★ ☆ ☆

RICH, MOIST AND FULL OF FLAVOR, THIS IS A DINNER-PARTY DELIGHT! GUESTS WILL LEAVE SMILING.

MAKES 12 SERVINGS | TOTAL PREP/COOK TIME: 1 HOUR **V**

INGREDIENTS

Cupcakes

· ¾ cup pastry flour (or substitute white whole-wheat flour)
· ½ cup natural granulated sugar ——
· ½ cup unsweetened cocoa powder
· 1 teaspoon baking powder
· 1 teaspoon baking soda
· ⅛ teaspoon salt
· ½ cup buttermilk
· ¼ cup light brown sugar ——
· 1 large egg, lightly beaten
· 2 tablespoons canola oil
· 2 teaspoons pure vanilla extract
· 2 teaspoons rum extract
· ½ cup hot strong coffee

[Z] Substitute ¼ cup + 2 tablespoons Stevia in the Raw® (or favorite no-calorie sweetener).

[Z] Substitute 1 cup date paste *(see "Great Dates," page 116).*

Sauce

· 1 large orange, juiced (about ½ cup)
· ½ cup confectioners' sugar
· 1 teaspoon rum
· 1 teaspoon pure vanilla extract
· 1 small orange, thinly sliced into 12 half-moons

DIRECTIONS

Cupcakes. Preheat the oven to 350°. Spray a 12-cup muffin pan with vegetable oil or insert cupcake liners. Whisk together the flour, sugar, cocoa, baking powder, baking soda and salt in a large bowl. Use an electric mixer to combine the buttermilk, brown sugar, egg, oil and vanilla and rum extracts. Add the dry ingredients and mix to combine. Add the hot coffee. The batter will be thin.

Pour the batter into the prepared pan. Bake until a tester inserted into the center of a cupcake comes out clean, about 15 to 20 minutes.

Sauce. Whisk the orange juice, confectioners' sugar, rum and vanilla extract in a deep pot over medium heat. Add the orange slices. Cook until the sugar dissolves and the flavors blend together, about 5 minutes.

To serve. Remove cupcake liners, if used, and place 1 cupcake on a dessert plate. Garnish with 1 cooked orange slice. Drizzle sauce on top and along the sides.

···

Per serving 135 calories, 3 grams total fat, 1 gram saturated fat, 2 grams monoun-saturated fat, 1 gram polyunsaturated fat, 16 milligrams cholesterol, 26 grams carbohydrates, 2 grams fiber, 3 grams protein, 186 milligrams sodium

➜ FLIP THE FRUIT

The rum sauce in this dessert is so versatile! Try modifying it with different fruits, such as mashed banana instead of orange juice and banana slices instead of orange slices.

TOSHA'S STORY
FINDING PURPOSE

I learned to cook from my mom. She was my heart—and losing her without warning to pneumonia took a toll on me mentally and physically. My weight soared to 215 pounds, and chronic migraines forced me to leave my law enforcement job.

It took time to accept that I needed a major lifestyle overhaul. I started reading magazine articles to learn about healthy living and changed my diet to include more whole grains, fruits and vegetables. Cutting out white bread and soda, skipping the fast food and walking three miles a day helped me lose 55 pounds. Walking also helped me deal with the sadness of losing my mom.

Enjoying life. Later, I found Zumba Fitness—the icing on my cake! The classes keep me on my weight-loss track, and I get so excited showing the dance moves to my husband. My motivation is remembering how I felt at my heaviest and how good I feel now.

Since deprivation diets don't work for me, I eat everything in moderation. I love to experiment with new recipes! And with the help of my neurologist, the migraines are under control.

Feeling fulfilled. Feeding mind, body and soul is critical. Volunteer work has given me a renewed sense of purpose, and I'm teaching Zumbatomic classes to help young people enjoy the same optimum health I do.

BE FRUITFUL
Try replacing the berries with peeled and chopped apples or other favorite fruits. Find more of Diana's original recipes at thechiclife.com.

MIXED-BERRY CRISP

FROM DIANA STEWART OF NORTH CAROLINA, USA

THIS SUMMERY DESSERT IS A CINCH TO MAKE!

MAKES 4 SERVINGS | TOTAL PREP/COOK TIME: 55 MINUTES **V**

★ ☆ ☆

INGREDIENTS

Berry Mix
· 4 cups fresh mixed berries (or substitute frozen berries, thawed)
· 2 teaspoons natural granulated sugar
· 1 teaspoon tapioca starch (or substitute cornstarch)
· ¼ teaspoon cinnamon

[Z] Substitute 2 teaspoons Stevia in the Raw® (or favorite no-calorie sweetener).

Topping
· ½ cup old-fashioned rolled oats
· ¼ cup whole-wheat flour
· 3 tablespoons brown sugar
· ¼ teaspoon cinnamon
· 3 tablespoons canola oil (or substitute coconut oil)
· ¼ cup walnuts or almonds, chopped (optional)

[Z] Substitute 3 tablespoons Stevia in the Raw® (or favorite no-calorie sweetener).

DIRECTIONS

Preheat the oven to 350°. In a bowl, combine the berry mix ingredients and stir. In a separate bowl, stir together the oats, flour, brown sugar and cinnamon. Work the oil into the dry mixture with a spoon or clean hands until it looks like wet sand. Stir in the nuts if using.

Coat a 7 x 11-inch or 8 x 8-inch baking pan with vegetable oil spray. Spread the berry mixture evenly to cover the bottom of the baking pan. Add the topping mix over the berries and spread it in an even layer. Bake 35 to 45 minutes, until top is lightly browned. Use an unslotted spatula or a large spoon to transfer servings to dessert bowls. Eat the crisp with a spoon.

....

Per serving 280 calories, 12 grams total fat, 1 gram saturated fat, 6.5 grams monounsaturated fat, 4 grams polyunsaturated fat, 0 milligrams cholesterol, 42 grams carbohydrates, 7 grams fiber, 3 grams protein, 85 milligrams sodium

FRUITY SUMMER GRANITA

FROM ASHLEY POUND OF PENNSYLVANIA, USA | EDITOR, *ZUMBA LOVERS COOKBOOK*

ON A HOT DAY, THIS ICY TREAT CAN'T BE BEAT!
MAKES 4 SERVINGS | TOTAL PREP/COOK TIME: 15 MINUTES PLUS 3 HOURS TO FREEZE **V**
★★★

INGREDIENTS

· 2 teaspoons loose peach white tea (or 1 tea bag)
· 2 cups frozen peach slices, partially thawed
  (or substitute fresh, in season)
· 1 cup frozen mango cubes, partially thawed
  (or substitute fresh, in season)
· ½ cup orange juice
· 2 teaspoons fresh ginger, finely grated
· ¼ teaspoon coarse salt
· 2 tablespoons fresh mint leaves, finely chopped
· 2 tablespoons agave nectar
· 1 tablespoon triple sec (optional)
· Whole mint leaves for garnish

DIRECTIONS

Steep the tea in 1 cup of boiling water, about 2 minutes. Discard the tea leaves or tea bag. Place the warm tea, peaches and mangoes in the bowl of a food processor and pulse until well mixed. Add the remaining ingredients and blend until smooth. Frozen peaches can vary in their tartness, so taste as you go, adjusting the amount of agave nectar to achieve a pleasing sweetness.

Pour the mixture into a freezer-safe glass bowl or baking dish and place in the freezer. After about 1 hour, use a fork to scrape the frozen surface into icy flakes. Cover with aluminum foil and freeze until firm, about 2 more hours. Scrape again until the granita is the consistency of a snow cone, breaking up any remaining chunks. Divide into individual glasses, garnish with mint leaves and eat with a spoon. Leftover granita can be covered and stored in the freezer for up to 3 days.

Per serving 100 calories, 0 grams total fat, 0 grams saturated fat, 0 grams monounsaturated fat, 0 grams polyunsaturated fat, 0 milligrams cholesterol, 24 grams carbohydrates, 2 grams fiber, 1 gram protein, 150 milligrams sodium

→ **COOL DOWN**
Refreshing granitas are made easily by combining any favorite fresh or frozen fruit with water and agave nectar or simple syrup. In Sicily, where granitas got their start, a creamier variety is made with ground almonds and fresh fruit and eaten with warm brioche for breakfast. Deliziosa!

PIÑA COLADA FROZEN YOGURT SANDWICHES

FROM CATHERINE DE ORIO OF ILLINOIS, USA | EDITOR-IN-CHIEF, CULINARYCURATOR.COM & GLAMOURGRUB.COM

IF YOU DON'T HAVE ALL DAY (AND WHO DOES?), YOU CAN MAKE THESE TROPICAL TREATS IN STAGES.

MAKES 12 SERVINGS | TOTAL PREP/COOK TIME: 1 HOUR, 10 MINUTES PLUS 5 TOTAL HOURS TO DRY PINEAPPLE AND FREEZE YOGURT Ⓥ

★☆☆

→ **SPECIAL EQUIPMENT**

You'll need an ice cream maker to whip up this delish dessert.

→ **ADVANCE PLANNING**

You can dry the pineapple slices ahead and store them in an airtight container for up to 3 days.

INGREDIENTS

Dried Pineapple Slices
· 1 medium pineapple, peeled, eyes removed, sliced into ¼-inch rounds (about 24 slices)

Frozen Yogurt
· 1 medium pineapple, peeled, cut into 1-inch cubes (about 3 cups)
· 1 cup cream of coconut
· ¼ cup natural granulated sugar —⌐ **[Z]** Substitute 2 tablespoons
· 2 tablespoons white rum   Stevia in the Raw® (or favorite
· 2 cups 2% Greek yogurt   no-calorie sweetener) + ½ cup
· 1 cup sweetened coconut flakes   unsweetened apple juice.

DIRECTIONS

Dried pineapple slices. Preheat the oven to 225°. Line a baking sheet with foil and place a cookie cooling rack on top. Gently pat the moist pineapple slices with paper towels until dry. On the cookie rack, place a single layer of slices without letting edges touch. Place the rack and cookie sheet in the oven and bake slices, flipping them once an hour for 3 to 4 hours until crisp and completely dry. Check often to avoid burning. Remove the slices from the oven and allow them to cool.

Frozen yogurt. You can prepare the frozen yogurt while waiting for the pineapple slices to bake and cool. Place the pineapple cubes and cream of coconut in a blender and purée until smooth. Transfer to a saucepan. Add the sugar and rum and cook over low heat, stirring until sugar is dissolved. Remove from heat and allow to cool.

In a bowl, whisk together the fruit purée, yogurt and coconut flakes. Transfer to an ice cream maker and churn per manufacturer's instructions. Churning in 2 batches may be necessary. Transfer the frozen yogurt to a metal container and freeze, about 3 to 4 hours or overnight.

Assembly. Remove the frozen yogurt from freezer and allow it to soften slightly. Place about ⅓ cup frozen yogurt onto 1 dried pineapple slice. Top with another slice and gently press until yogurt spreads to the edge of the slices. Repeat with remaining pineapple slices and frozen yogurt. Serve immediately or wrap each sandwich in plastic wrap and freeze for up to 1 week.

....

Per serving 217 calories, 6 grams total fat, 5 grams saturated fat, 0 grams monounsaturated fat, 0 grams polyunsaturated fat, 0 milligrams cholesterol, 38.5 grams carbohydrates, 2.5 grams fiber, 3 grams protein, 78 milligrams sodium

ON THE GO

EASY ENERGY BOOSTERS

These übernutritious yummies will give you the fuel you need to get moving without weighing you down.

Smoothies. Want a simple way to get more veggies in your diet? Befriend your blender! Blending and drinking fruit with greens and other vegetables can help you reach your recommended daily intake faster and may help your body absorb the nutrients more easily.

Breads & Granolas. If you've been scanning labels, you know most of the granolas and snack bars on supermarket shelves are no healthier than candy. Try making them at home. When you mix them up yourself, you get everything you want—and nothing you don't. The granolas and breakfast breads in this section are perfect for morning or midday snacks or a quick bite before Zumba class.

....

★★★ **ZUMBA ALL-STARS**
★★☆ **OCCASIONAL EATS**
★☆☆ **SOMETIME SPLURGES**

SMOOTHIES

→ **GO "PRO"**
*Look for yogurt
with live, active
cultures, the
probiotics that
help improve
digestive health.*

TROPICAL BERRY SMOOTHIE

FROM MINDY BELCHER OF GEORGIA, USA

*AMP UP THE PROTEIN WITH GREEK YOGURT OR SKIP
THE YOGURT FOR A LIGHTER, VEGAN OPTION—
THE BANANA AND ICE MAKE THE DRINK CREAMY.*
MAKES 2 SERVINGS | TOTAL PREP TIME: 10 MINUTES **V**
★★★

INGREDIENTS
· 1 cup plain nonfat yogurt
· ½ cup orange juice
· 1 medium mango, peeled, pitted, diced (about 1 cup)
  (or substitute frozen mango chunks)
· 1 cup mixed berries (such as strawberries and blueberries)
· ½ medium banana
· ½ teaspoon pure vanilla extract

DIRECTIONS
Place the yogurt, orange juice, mango, mixed berries,
banana and vanilla extract in a blender with a few ice cubes.
Pulse to emulsify.

....

*Per serving 210 calories, 1 gram total fat, 0 grams saturated fat,
0 grams monounsaturated fat, 0 grams polyunsaturated fat,
0 milligrams cholesterol, 47 grams carbohydrates, 6 grams fiber,
7 grams protein, 61 milligrams sodium*

JUDITH'S STORY
OPPOSITES ATTRACT

My husband and I have different approaches to eating. I like homemade foods using fresh ingredients and very little sugar, and I make my own soups and stocks.

My husband, on the other hand, likes processed foods, frozen pizzas and canned soups. As a Japanese-American, he feels he has to have white rice at nearly every meal, while I prefer the brown variety—causing more than a few "rice wars" in our household. As an Italian, I'm used to cooking with tomatoes all the time. My husband—who didn't grow up eating them—is not a fan.

Common ground. After 20 years of marriage, we've found ways to compromise. I do most of the cooking, and he supplements with his favorite foods. But one thing we've always agreed on is our Zumba classes. He takes them at the office gym, and I go after I drop the kids at school. It's how we both stay fit despite our different eating habits.

Ready for anything. Another way for me to stay healthy is to be prepared. That means starting the day with a good breakfast—steel-cut oats and yogurt. And I take along hummus, carrots or bananas to the gym so I don't rely on vending-machine snacks after class.

I guess my habits are paying off. My doctor tells me I have the heart of a 38-year-old—and I'm 57!

MATCHA SMOOTHIE

FROM JUDITH MACK OF ALASKA, USA

MAKE THIS PROTEIN-RICH SMOOTHIE IN MINUTES!
MAKES 2 SERVINGS | TOTAL PREP TIME: 5 MINUTES Ⓥ
★★★

INGREDIENTS
· 2 cups unsweetened almond milk (such as Almond Breeze® brand)
· 2 tablespoons agave nectar (or substitute honey)
· 1 tablespoon matcha green tea powder
· 1 tablespoon protein powder
· 1 tablespoon ground flaxseeds or whole chia seeds (optional)

DIRECTIONS
Place all of the ingredients into a blender. Add about 2 cups of ice cubes. Blend until smooth.

Per serving 133 calories, 5 grams total fat, 0 grams saturated fat, 2.5 grams monounsaturated fat, 1 gram polyunsaturated fat, 0 milligrams cholesterol, 22 grams carbohydrates, 2 grams fiber, 4 grams protein, 196 milligrams sodium

WHY USE POWDER?

Green tea powder packs about 10 times more powerful polyphenol antioxidants than a cup of steeped green tea and has been linked to health benefits, including cancer prevention and improved bone health. Matcha tea—a very mild blend of green tea—is traditional in Japan and found in specialty tea stores or online.

MEXICAN SMOOTHIE

FROM LINDSEY CHAQUETTE OF OREGON, USA

ADDING A SHOT OF COOLED ESPRESSO MAKES THIS A MEXICAN MOCHA.

MAKES 2 SERVINGS | TOTAL PREP TIME: 5 MINUTES ⒱

★★☆

INGREDIENTS
· ¾ cup plain nonfat Greek yogurt
· ¼ cup vanilla whey protein powder
· 1 tablespoon cocoa powder
· 1 teaspoon pure vanilla extract
· 2 tablespoons agave nectar (or substitute sugar-free plain or vanilla syrup)
· ¼ teaspoon cinnamon

DIRECTIONS
Place all of the ingredients into a blender. Add ice cubes and blend until smooth.

....

Per serving 176 calories, 1 gram total fat, 0 grams saturated fat, 0 grams monounsaturated fat, 0 grams polyunsaturated fat, 0 milligrams cholesterol, 29 grams carbohydrates, 1 gram fiber, 16 grams protein, 105 milligrams sodium

ACTION-PACKED SMOOTHIE

FROM ANGELA ANDERSON OF COLORADO, USA

GOING GREEN NEVER TASTED SO GOOD!

MAKES 2 SERVINGS | TOTAL PREP TIME: 15 MINUTES ⒱ 🌶

★★★

INGREDIENTS
· 2 oranges, peeled, divided into sections, seeds removed
· 1 lemon, peeled, divided into sections, seeds removed
· 1 apple, peeled, cored, quartered
· 1 banana, peeled
· 1 (1- to 2-inch) piece fresh ginger, peeled and sliced
· 1 cup fresh parsley
· 1-3 leaves kale, spines removed, chopped (about 1 cup)
· ½ cup fresh mint (or substitute with basil)

DIRECTIONS
Place the oranges, lemon, apple, banana and ginger into a blender. Pulse to emulsify. Add enough water to just cover the ingredients. Blend on the low setting, slowly adding the parsley, kale and mint. Add ice cubes if desired. Blend until smooth.

....

Per serving 227 calories, 2 grams total fat, 0 grams saturated fat, 0 grams monounsaturated fat, 0 grams polyunsaturated fat, 0 milligrams cholesterol, 54 grams carbohydrates, 11 grams fiber, 6 grams protein, 45 milligrams sodium

➜ **SPICE IT UP!**
Add ginger. It can make you feel more alert, and it's known for easing stress. Plus, ginger improves circulation to help vitamins reach every part of your body!

APPLE OATMEAL BREAD

FROM EDIT GERGELY OF HARGHITA, ROMANIA

THIS NOT-TOO-SWEET BREAD IS A TREAT FOR WEEKEND MORNINGS.

MAKES 12 SERVINGS | *TOTAL PREP/COOK TIME: 1 HOUR, 15 MINUTES* **V**

★ ★ ☆

INGREDIENTS

· 2½ cups whole-wheat flour
· 2 tablespoons old-fashioned rolled oats
· 1 teaspoon baking powder
· 1 teaspoon baking soda
· 1 teaspoon cinnamon
· ½ teaspoon salt
· 2 tablespoons natural granulated sugar
· 4 eggs
· ½ cup vegetable oil (or substitute coconut oil)
· 3 medium apples, peeled, cored, grated
  (about 3 cups)
· 1 teaspoon pure vanilla extract

[Z] Substitute 2 tablespoons Stevia in the Raw® (or favorite no-calorie sweetener).

DIRECTIONS

Preheat the oven to 350°. Whisk together the flour, oats, baking powder, baking soda, cinnamon and salt in a small bowl. In a large bowl, use an electric mixer to combine the sugar, eggs, vegetable oil and vanilla extract. Add the dry ingredients to the wet mixture. Stir in the apples.

Pour the batter into a 9 x 5-inch loaf pan coated with vegetable oil spray. Bake until a tester inserted in the center of the loaf comes out clean, about 45 minutes to 1 hour.

Per serving 156 calories, 3 grams total fat, 2 grams saturated fat, 1 gram monoun-saturated fat, trace amount polyunsaturated fat, 62 milligrams cholesterol, 27 grams carbohydrates, 2 grams fiber, 5 grams protein, 253 milligrams sodium

→ SWEET TOOTH?
Slather on a heaping teaspoon of natural, unsweetened apple butter, found in many groceries and farmers' markets.

BREADS & GRANOLAS

BLUEBERRY OAT MUFFINS

FROM JANINE KOUTSKY OF PENNSYLVANIA, USA

GRAB ONE OF THESE MOIST, TASTY TREATS BEFORE A WORKOUT.

MAKES 18 SERVINGS | TOTAL PREP/COOK TIME: 1 HOUR **V**

★ ★ ★

INGREDIENTS

· 2 tablespoons silken tofu
· 3 large bananas, mashed
· 1 egg (or egg substitute)
· 3 tablespoons sunflower oil
· ⅓ cup honey
· 1¼ cups whole-wheat pastry flour
· 1 tablespoon soy flour
· ½ cup oat bran
· 2 teaspoons baking powder
· ½ teaspoon baking soda
· 1 teaspoon ground cinnamon
· ½ teaspoon salt
· 2 cups blueberries, fresh or frozen

DIRECTIONS

Preheat the oven to 375°. Combine the tofu, mashed bananas, egg, oil and honey in a mixing bowl. Mix on low speed with an electric mixer. Add flours, oat bran, baking powder, baking soda, cinnamon and salt, continuing on low speed until mixed. Stir in the blueberries. (TIP: If using frozen berries, coat them first with flour to keep muffins from turning purple.)

Line an 18-cup muffin tin with cupcake liners. Spoon the batter into liners until each is about ⅔ full. Bake for 25 to 30 minutes, until golden.

Per serving 110 calories, 3 grams total fat, 0 grams saturated fat, .5 gram monounsaturated fat, 1.5 grams polyunsaturated fat, 10 milligrams cholesterol, 21 grams carbohydrates, 3 grams fiber, 3 grams protein, 270 milligrams sodium

➜ **GO FOR THE O!**
Add chopped walnuts, ground flaxseeds or flaxseed oil—all good omega-3 sources.

OATMEAL BREAKFAST COOKIES
FROM LISA BLUHM OF WASHINGTON, USA

THIS NUTRITIOUS COOKIE IS A GREAT ON-THE-GO SNACK. YOU CAN EASILY INCREASE THE RECIPE TO MAKE BIGGER BATCHES AND STORE EXTRAS IN THE FREEZER.

MAKES 4 SERVINGS | TOTAL PREP/COOK TIME: 20 MINUTES V
★★★

INGREDIENTS
· 1 cup old-fashioned rolled oats
· 2 egg whites
· 2 tablespoons honey
· ½ teaspoon pumpkin pie spice
· ¼ cup canned pumpkin purée (or substitute ½ cup natural, unsweetened applesauce or 1 mashed banana)
· 1 tablespoon dark chocolate chips (optional)
· 1 tablespoon chopped nuts (optional)

DIRECTIONS
Preheat the oven to 350°. Combine the oats, egg whites, honey, pumpkin pie spice and pumpkin purée in a bowl. Add any of the optional ingredients to the cookie batter.

Use a small ice cream scoop to mound the dough onto a baking sheet. Use the bottom of a glass to flatten the cookies to about ½-inch thickness. Bake until golden, about 12 minutes.

Per serving 121 calories, 1.5 grams total fat, .5 gram saturated fat, .5 gram monounsaturated fat, .5 gram polyunsaturated fat, 0 milligrams cholesterol, 23 grams carbohydrates, 2.5 grams fiber, 5 grams protein, 29 milligrams sodium

→ **SUGAR-FREE SOLUTION**
You can substitute up to 15 drops of plain or vanilla liquid stevia for the honey.

"To avoid boring meals, I'll eat lunch for breakfast or breakfast for dinner, and I'm always looking for fun recipes to tweak." —LISA

CHEWY CRANBERRY OATMEAL BARS

INSPIRED BY A RECIPE FROM CRYSTAL CLARK OF ILLINOIS, USA

MAKE THESE YUMMY BARS AHEAD AND HAVE ONE READY TO GO FOR A QUICK BREAKFAST.

MAKES 12 SERVINGS | TOTAL PREP/COOK TIME: 40 MINUTES **V**
★★★

INGREDIENTS
- 1½ cups white whole-wheat flour
- 1 teaspoon baking soda
- 1½ teaspoons ground cinnamon
- ¼ cup + 3 tablespoons Stevia in the Raw® (or favorite no-calorie sweetener)
- 2 medium ripe bananas
- 1 cup plain nonfat Greek yogurt
- 2 egg whites, lightly beaten
- 2 tablespoons canola oil
- 2 tablespoons milk
- 2 teaspoons pure vanilla extract
- 3 cups old-fashioned rolled oats
- 1 cup dried cranberries

DIRECTIONS
Preheat the oven to 350°. Whisk together the flour, baking soda and ground cinnamon in a small bowl. Use an electric mixer to combine the stevia, bananas, yogurt, egg whites, oil, milk and vanilla extract. Add the dry ingredients to the wet ingredients and mix. Stir in the oats and cranberries. Spread into an ungreased 13 x 9-inch pan and bake until golden, about 25 to 30 minutes. Cool and cut into bars.

....

Per serving 209 calories, 5 grams total fat, .5 gram saturated fat, 2 grams monounsaturated fat, 1.5 grams polyunsaturated fat, 1 milligram cholesterol, 37 grams carbohydrates, 4 grams fiber, 7 grams protein, 130 milligrams sodium

GUILTLESS GRANOLA

FROM GILLIE TICE OF DELAWARE, USA

SERVE OVER PLAIN GREEK YOGURT WITH A DRIZZLE OF HONEY FOR A GO-TO SNACK BEFORE ZUMBA CLASS.
MAKES 24 SERVINGS | *TOTAL PREP/COOK TIME: 40 MINUTES* **V**
★★★

INGREDIENTS
· 3 cups old-fashioned rolled oats
· 1½ cups nutty cereal (such as Grape Nuts® brand)
· 1 cup sliced raw almonds
· ½ cup milled flaxseeds
· ½ cup wheat bran
· 1 cup low-fat powdered milk
  (or substitute nonfat powdered milk)
· 1 teaspoon cinnamon
· ½ teaspoon sea salt
· ½ cup pure maple syrup
· 4 tablespoons canola oil

[Z] Substitute 1 tablespoon Stevia in the Raw® (or favorite no-calorie sweetener).

DIRECTIONS
Preheat the oven to 325°. Combine all of the dry ingredients in a large bowl. Whisk together the maple syrup and oil. Pour the wet ingredients over the dry ingredients and toss well. The granola will be slightly sticky. Spread the mix onto 2 baking sheets coated with vegetable oil spray. Bake, using a spatula to loosen and turn the granola every 5 minutes, until golden, about 20 to 30 minutes. Remove from the oven and cool to room temperature. Divide the granola into 24 resealable bags for individual portions or store in 1 large airtight container.

Per serving *156 calories, 6 grams total fat, .5 gram saturated fat, 3.5 grams monounsaturated fat, 2 grams polyunsaturated fat, 1 milligram cholesterol, 21.5 grams carbohydrates, 3 grams fiber, 5 grams protein, 121 milligrams sodium*

CHOCOLATE GRANOLA PICK-ME-UP

FROM ANGELA GLUCK OF FLORIDA, USA

GRAB A HANDFUL AND GO!
MAKES 8 SERVINGS | *TOTAL PREP/COOK TIME: 30 MINUTES* **V**
★★☆

INGREDIENTS
· 2 tablespoons natural brown sugar
· 1 teaspoon olive oil
· ½ teaspoon pure vanilla extract
· 2 tablespoons honey
· 1-2 tablespoons chocolate protein powder
· 1 tablespoon unsweetened cocoa powder
· 2 cups old-fashioned rolled oats

DIRECTIONS
Preheat the oven to 350°. Place 3 tablespoons water into a bowl. Stir in the sugar, oil, vanilla extract and honey. Mix in the protein powder and cocoa powder. Add the oats and stir until they are covered well. Spread mixture onto a baking sheet coated with vegetable oil spray. Bake, turning once, until the oats are brown and crispy, 15 to 20 minutes.

Per serving *118 calories, 2 grams total fat, .5 gram saturated fat, 1 gram monounsaturated fat, 1 gram polyunsaturated fat, 0 milligrams cholesterol, 24 grams carbohydrates, 2 grams fiber, 3.5 grams protein, 10 milligrams sodium*

→ **GREAT GIFT**
Seal granola in colorful bags and give them to your Zumba pals!

"You have to look at food as your building blocks. Ask yourself, 'Is this the best-quality material I can give my body to keep me fit?'" —GILLIE

CRUNCHY GRANOLA BARS

FROM MINDY BELCHER OF GEORGIA, USA

MIX AND MATCH WHATEVER CEREALS, NUTS AND SEEDS YOU HAVE ON HAND TO MAKE THESE NO-BAKE SNACK BARS.

MAKES 16 SERVINGS | TOTAL PREP TIME: 10 MINUTES PLUS 30 MINUTES TO REFRIGERATE **V**

★★★

INGREDIENTS

· 2 cups whole-grain crunchy cereal
  (such as Grape Nuts® brand)
· ½ cup fiber cereal, crushed
  (such as Fiber One® brand)
· ¼ cup ground flaxseeds
· ¼ cup vanilla protein powder
· ¼ cup sunflower seeds
· ¼ cup millet
· ¼ cup steel-cut oats
· ¾ cup honey
· ¼ cup peanut butter
· 1 cup dried fruit or chocolate
  chips (optional)

DIRECTIONS

Place the cereals, flaxseeds, protein powder, sunflower seeds, millet and oats into a bowl. Soften the honey and peanut butter in a microwave oven until smooth, about 2 to 3 minutes. Pour into the bowl. Add the dried fruit or chocolate if using. Use a wooden spoon to combine the mixture.

Spread into a baking sheet coated with vegetable oil spray. Cover and refrigerate for 30 minutes to set the bars. Cut into 16 pieces.

....

Per serving 190 calories, 9 grams total fat, 3 grams saturated fat, 3 grams monounsaturated fat, 2 grams polyunsaturated fat, 2 milligrams cholesterol, 28 grams carbohydrates, 2 grams fiber, 4 grams protein, 30 milligrams sodium

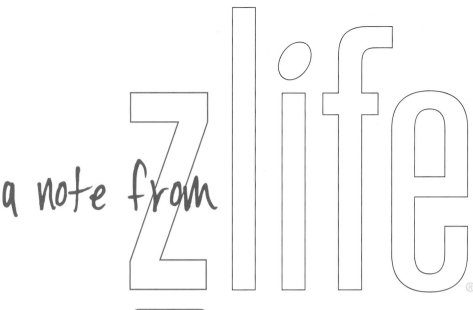

a note from zlife®

▸▸ BRING THE EXCITEMENT

Being a part of the Zumba Fitness community means more than just strutting your stuff on the dance floor. It means dedicating yourself to a life full of energy, excitement and positivity with a focus on overall health. It means taking the sense of joy and exhilaration that you find within a class and translating it into all aspects of your life—from beauty and wellness to style, travel and nutrition. It means becoming a part of a global family striving to live a true Z-LIFE.

Want more? Bring the fun and infectious energy of Zumba Fitness directly into your home by joining our party in print! Visit **zlifemag.com** and subscribe to *Z-LIFE* magazine today. Get fabulous recipes like the ones seen here as well as the latest in style, health, beauty and music.

Become a part of the Zumba community through *Z-LIFE*. We can't wait to welcome you!

Andrea

Andrea Carneiro
Editor-in-Chief, *Z-LIFE* Magazine

BIOS & ACKNOWLEDGMENTS

thanks to...

ASHLEY POUND
EDITOR & PUBLISHER

Ashley is a veteran of the New York publishing industry and worked with Zumba Fitness to create *Z-LIFE* magazine as its founding editor-in-chief. Her company, Ashley Pound Creative (ashleypound.com), produces and publishes custom content, design and photography for magazines, websites and social media. She is a vegetarian and has had a lifelong fascination with nutrition and healthy-eating trends.

MOLLY MORGAN, RD, CDN, CSSD
NUTRITION ADVISER

Molly is a board-certified sports specialist dietitian and the author of *The Skinny Rules: The 101 Secrets Every Skinny Girl Knows*. Her company, Creative Nutrition Solutions, has developed nutrition programs for pro sports teams and Fortune 500 companies, and she has been featured on CNN and in national fitness and lifestyle magazines. She blogs about health and nutrition at creativenutritionsolutions.com.

ANASTASIA CONOVER, MS, RD, CDN, CNSC
NUTRITION ADVISER

Anastasia is a certified personal trainer, dietitian and owner of the nutrition and fitness consultancy Just Nutritious. She offers online tools for healthy eating and blogs about nutrition at justnutritious.com. Anastasia created the accelerated weight-loss plan for the Zumba DVD series *Exhilarate!* and the official pink "Z" tips throughout this book.

THE ZUMBA® LOVERS who submitted recipes for consideration in this cookbook. Your enthusiasm for living and eating well is an inspiration! We hope you'll continue to share your tips and recipes with the worldwide Zumba® community through *Z-LIFE*™ magazine and zlifemag.com. Write to editorial@zlifemag.com.

LAUREN SOMERS and **SUSANNAH FELTS,** who interviewed recipe authors and helped us share their favorite healthy-eating tips and personal stories.

JORJ MORGAN, author of many cookbooks, who contributed cooking tips and worked on the initial formatting, modification and testing of recipes—along with her team of testers: Nancy Dougherty, Rose Dreyfus, P.J. Forbes, Cindy Greenberg, Mindy Hanna, Rose Hegele, Gail Jordan, Amy Kendall, Jessica Kettler, Sue Kline, Lydia LaRocca, Mel Lemm, Mary Lester, Bunnie Look, Kate McLaine, Sharon Murrah, April L. Nosek, Jane Palmisano, Louise Proffer, Maureen Rotella, Diana Shelton, Sandra Shu, Geri Seinberg and Mel Sirois.

JANINE KOUTSKY, MS, Zumba® instructor, wellness counselor and nutrition educator, who contributed research, tips, recipe testing and laughs.

ANNA BERMAN, recipe developer and blogger at snackinginthekitchen.com, for additional recipe testing and modification.

SANDRA BAN and **LAUREN SOMERS** for skilled copy editing and proofreading.

The Zumba Fitness® team:

BETTY McGUINNESS, Publisher of *Z-LIFE*™ magazine, who led as team liaison.

HILARY FITCH, Executive Creative Director, who directed the gorgeous photography and design.

SARAH RUSIN, Designer, who did a beautiful job creating the look of this book.

JEFFREY PERLMAN, Chief Marketing Officer, and **ADELE HARRINGTON,** VP of Global Consumer Products, for being game to try anything.

DAVID TOPEL, Community Manager, **ILIANA SOTO,** Social Media Coordinator, and **CLAUDIA ALGAZE,** Manager of Global Consumer Products, for being a bridge to Zumba® lovers everywhere.

SCOTT CHITOFF, Chief Legal Officer, for his expertise.

RONIT SHLESINGER, Traffic Manager, for talking softly and carrying a big pink stick.

Ashley

GLOSSARY & SUBSTITUTIONS

What's Enemy No. 1 when it comes to working out? Boredom! That's why we change up the moves and add our own flavor—to keep exercise from feeling routine. The same goes for cooking. Here, and throughout the book, you'll find wildly different flavors to expand your palate, plus substitutions and tips to inspire your creativity and make these dishes your own.

A

AGAR-AGAR POWDER – See "Thickeners."

AGAVE NECTAR, ORGANIC – See "Sugar & Substitutes."

ANCHO CHILE PEPPER – The ancho (AHN-choh) is a dried red poblano chile that adds a sweet, slightly sharp flavor and moderate heat to sauces, soups, marinades, rubs and tamales.

ANTIOXIDANTS – Antioxidants are vitamins, minerals and other nutrients that protect and repair cells from damage caused by free radicals—organic molecules thought to contribute to tissue damage, aging and a range of chronic diseases. The three major antioxidant vitamins are beta-carotene, vitamin C and vitamin E, which may help keep the immune system strong. Get them by eating plenty of colorful fruits and vegetables.

B

BABY SWEET CORN – Popular in Asian cooking, these tiny cobs of corn are sold canned or frozen and eaten whole.

BAKING POWDER & BAKING SODA – While both help baked foods rise, baking *soda* is activated by acid—better suited for recipes with an acidic ingredient or two; baking *powder* has acid built in and works best with nonacidic ingredients.

BALSAMIC VINEGAR – True *balsamicos* are made in Italy with white trebbiano grapes, but what passes in the U.S. for balsamic vinegar (concentrated, lightly sweetened red wine vinegar) is a good, lower-cost option. In addition to adding complex flavor to fruit, chocolate sauce or grilled vegetables, balsamic vinegar is best known for its starring role in oil-based vinaigrettes. It can also hold its own—without oil or added sugar—as a low-calorie (about 15 per tablespoon), nonfat salad dressing.

BELL PEPPER – Decked out in brilliant orange, red, yellow or green, bell peppers have little to no heat. They're low in calories, fat and sodium, high in fiber and rich in antioxidants.

BROWN SUGAR – See "Sugar & Substitutes."

BULGUR – This whole-wheat Middle Eastern staple is served like rice and is a low-fat source of protein, minerals and fiber.

BUTTER & SUBSTITUTES – Dairy butter is loved for its flavor and texture but not for its high levels of dietary cholesterol and saturated fat. Margarine and "buttery spreads" made from vegetable oil have no cholesterol, but some contain trans fat—not a heart-healthy trade-off. To avoid trans fat, pass up brands with "hydrogenated" in the ingredients. Use butter or margarine—each about 100 calories per tablespoon—sparingly.

To reduce calories and saturated fat, try cutting half the butter called for in a recipe or substitute half the butter with an equal amount of unsweetened applesauce, puréed prunes (best for chocolate and spiced cakes) or puréed pumpkin (ideal for spiced breads, cakes, muffins and quick breads). For table use, opt for whipped butter or whipped buttery spreads. Earth Balance®, for example, offers a whipped, vegan spread with 20 fewer calories and 4.5 fewer grams of saturated fat per tablespoon than butter and no trans fat. Butter blends (real butter mixed with canola or olive oil) also have less saturated fat than pure butter, and some may be lower in calories. Certain varieties are appropriate for baking (see *product websites for guidance*). You can also try spreads that contain plant-based stanols or sterols to help block the body's absorption of cholesterol, such as Benecol®.

C

CAYENNE CHILE PEPPER – Cayenne (CAH-yehn) chiles are long, thin and red and fall on the heat scale between serranos and habañeros. See also "Red Chile Pepper."

CEVICHE (OR SEVICHE) – Ceviche (seh-VEE-cheh) is popular in coastal regions of South and Central America and typically includes one or more raw seafood items. Marinated in a citrus-based mixture, the seafood becomes "denatured"— essentially cooked enough to kill any bacteria.

CHEESE & SUBSTITUTES – Cheese is a good source of protein and calcium, but it can also be high in cholesterol and saturated fat. Regular cheddar, for example, has about 9 grams of fat per ounce—two-thirds of it saturated. Aim for quality over quantity. Aged cheeses such as Parmesan, extra-sharp cheddar and Asiago offer lots of flavor, so you only need small amounts to accent a meal. Cheeses that are naturally lower in fat—farmer's cheese, Neufchâtel, cottage cheese and yogurt cheese—can be used to add creamy texture. Reduced-fat versions of cheeses, such as Monterey Jack, mozzarella, brie, Swiss, Muenster and colby, cut fat by one-fourth and calories by up to one-third. See also "Feta Cheese."

NONDAIRY CHEESE. Make a no-cholesterol, lower-fat vegan tofu ricotta (see page 84), or cube and season firm tofu to replace paneer, a soft-curd cheese, in Indian dishes. Substitute Parmesan with cheesy-tasting nutritional yeast—high in fiber, B vitamins and protein, low in fat and sodium—on pizza and popcorn and in sauces and pesto. Or blend nutritional yeast with agar-agar, nuts and other ingredients to make your own mozzarella, cheddar and other nondairy cheeses.

CHICKPEAS (OR GARBANZO BEANS) – A staple in Middle Eastern, Mediterranean, South American and vegetarian cuisines, chickpeas are a source of dietary fiber, protein, iron and other minerals. See also "Meat & Substitutes."

CHILE PEPPER – Chiles add varying levels of heat to dishes. See "Ancho," "Cayenne," "Habañero," "Jalapeño," "Poblano" or "Red" Chile Pepper for details. *(Continued)*

CHILI POWDER – Chili powder is a blend of dried chiles and ground spices used to add flavor to burritos, chili and rubs.

CILANTRO (OR CHINESE PARSLEY) – Commonly used in Asian, Mexican and Indian cuisines, cilantro *(sil-AHN-troh)* is a pungent herb that complements spicy foods. In the U.S., "cilantro" refers to the leaves and stems of the coriander plant, and "coriander" refers to its seeds. *See also "Coriander."*

COARSE SALT (OR KOSHER SALT) – In this book, "coarse salt" refers to sea salt or kosher salt, which has a larger grain than table salt. Those bigger bits, when used as a garnish, make the saltiness more pronounced, so a little goes a long way. While finer salt is best for baking, coarse salt is a favorite for cooking and seasoning because it's easy to handle. Both varieties have equal amounts of sodium, but table salt is typically iodized and more refined. *See also "Salt & Substitutes."*

COCONUT MILK – See "Milk & Substitutes."

CORIANDER – Coriander *(KOHR-ee-an-der)* seeds have a spicy, lemony aroma and are used in spice blends that include curry powders and chili powders. *See also "Cilantro."*

CREAM OF COCONUT – This is the sugar-sweetened coconut cream used in piña coladas—not to be confused with the unsweetened coconut cream or milk used in Thai curries.

CREAM SUBSTITUTES – If you want the richness or texture of dairy cream with fewer calories and less saturated fat or cholesterol, try these options: Evaporated skim milk, half-and-half or blended silken tofu can replace heavy cream in some dishes. In cream-based soup or sauce recipes, swap cream for cooked-and-puréed navy beans, split peas, peeled russet potatoes or sweet potatoes. In both sweet and savory dishes, try creamed avocado or oat cream to add richness.

CUMIN (OR COMINO) – Cumin *(KOO-muhn)*, the dried seeds of a plant of the parsley family, is ground and added to curries and savory spice blends used to season fish, lamb, lentils and more.

CURRY POWDER, BOTTLED – Commercially bottled curry powder is not as complex as the custom blends of about 20 freshly ground spices used in India. Many bottled curry powders start with a base of ground red chiles, coriander and cumin and are then customized with additional spices—such as cardamom, fenugreek, turmeric, garlic or cinnamon.

D

DATE SUGAR – See "Sugar & Substitutes."

DIETARY FIBER (OR ROUGHAGE OR BULK) – Dietary fiber includes the parts of whole grains, vegetables, fruits, beans, legumes and nuts that resist digestion in the gastrointestinal tract. Fiber helps move material through the digestive system. *See also "Take care of your heart," page 14.*

E

EGG & SUBSTITUTES – An egg has as much protein as an ounce of red meat. The yolk has B vitamins and all the essential amino acids, but it also has two-thirds of the maximum recommended cholesterol for a day. Here are a few alternatives: Swap 1 whole egg for 2 egg whites or ¼ cup liquid egg substitute such as Egg Beaters® to get an equal amount of protein, cut the calories in half and eliminate the cholesterol.

The fewer eggs called for in a recipe, the easier it is to replace them. When substituting in baking, add a pinch of baking powder or baking soda, depending on the dish, to make it light and fluffy. *See also "Baking Powder & Baking Soda."*

EGG-FREE ALTERNATIVES. If avoiding animal products, you can try swapping 1 whole egg for one of the following in baked or cooked dishes: a) ¼ cup unsweetened puréed apricots, prunes, pumpkin, squash or applesauce, depending on flavors in the dish; b) ground flaxseeds mixed with water *(see "Flaxseeds")*; c) 1 small mashed banana (about ½ cup); d) 1½ teaspoons Ener-G Egg Replacer® mixed with 2 tablespoons water; e) 1½ tablespoons soy lecithin granules mixed with 2 teaspoons water; f) ¼ cup whipped silken tofu (for simulating custardy quiches or replacing eggs in dense baked goods). Replace 1 egg white with 1 tablespoon agar-agar powder mixed with 1 tablespoon cold water. For mock scrambles, replace each egg with ¼ cup firm, crumbled tofu and flavor with curry spices or prepared seasoning. For a vegan yolk replacement, try The Vegg®, a no-cholesterol substitute made with nutritional yeast and black sea salt. *See also "Thickeners."*

F

FETA CHEESE – A staple in Greece, feta *(FEH-tuh)* has a a rich, salty taste and a crumbly texture and is lower in fat and calories than most whole-milk cheeses. If bought in brick form, soak feta in water a few minutes to reduce the sodium. Rinse and dry.

FLAXSEEDS, BLENDED WITH WATER – Flaxseeds are an excellent source of omega-3 fatty acids, particularly for those who don't eat fish. They also have binding properties when blended with water. For the equivalent of 1 egg, grind 1 heaping tablespoon of whole flaxseeds until fine (or use 2 tablespoons prepared, ground seeds), combine with ¼ cup cold water and blend 2 to 3 minutes. Let rest about 3 minutes to thicken.

G

GARAM MASALA – Garam masala *(GAHR-uhm muh-SAH-luh)* is a ground Indian spice blend that fills your kitchen with the heady aromas of cumin, coriander, cardamom and cinnamon. Discover recipes online to make your own or find bottled versions in markets that carry a wide selection of spices.

GARBANZO BEANS (OR CHICKPEAS) – See "Chickpeas."

GLUTEN & GLUTEN-FREE – Gluten is a protein found in wheat, barley, rye and some oat products. Many prepared "gluten-free" products have added sugar and fat, so check labels.

GLYCEMIC INDEX – The glycemic index (GI) ranks specific carbohydrates from 0 to 100 based on how they release glucose into the bloodstream. The faster glucose is released, the higher the food's GI—meaning more insulin is released to keep blood sugar stable. Learn more and see how foods rate on the glycemic (glahy-SEE-mic) index at glycemicindex.com.

GNOCCHI – Gnocchi (NYAW-kee) are small Italian dumplings typically made from potatoes and served like pasta with sauce.

GREEK YOGURT, PLAIN – Greek yogurt goes through a straining process, which makes it thicker and creamier than regular yogurt. The Greek variety can also have less lactose, half the carbs, half the sodium and as much as twice the protein. Find nonfat and reduced-fat versions in most groceries. Eat Greek yogurt topped with fresh fruit or granola or use it as a lower-fat substitute for sour cream or mayonnaise.

H

HABAÑERO CHILE PEPPER – The habañero (hah-bahn-YEH-roh) is Mexico's hottest chile pepper, starting out green and turning orange, red, brown or white as it matures. Its fruity flavor complements fresh salsas made with tropical fruits.

HOAGIE – The hoagie (HOH-gee) originated in Philadelphia, Pennsylvania, and is typically layered with meat, cheese, lettuce and tomatoes. Locals claim that it's unique among submarine sandwiches for its special Italian baked bread, oil and herbs.

HONEY – See "Sugar & Substitutes."

J

JALAPEÑO CHILE PEPPER – Whether raw, dry or pickled, this dark green chile—popular in Mexican and U.S. Southwest cooking—brings flavor and medium heat to salsas and sauces. A smoked jalapeño (hah-luh-PEHN-yoh) is known as a chipotle.

JASMINE RICE (OR THAI FRAGRANT RICE) – This long-grain rice clings but is less sticky than some rices. It has a nutty taste and floral aroma. A whole-grain (brown) version can be found in some markets and online.

K

KOSHER SALT – See "Coarse Salt."

L

LEGUMES – Legumes, including beans, lentils, peanuts, peas and soybeans, are a rich source of protein and other nutrients. See also "Meat & Substitutes."

M

MAPLE SYRUP – See "Sugar & Substitutes."

MEAT & SUBSTITUTES – Red meat, pork, poultry and seafood are referred to generically as "meat" when distinguishing them from vegetarian or vegan ingredients in this book. The term "meatless" identifies dishes that do not contain animal flesh or byproducts—such as chicken stock—but may include dairy and eggs. See also "Vegan" and "Vegetarian, Ovo-Lacto."

Health-conscious meat eaters can cut back on saturated fat and cholesterol by trimming solid fat before cooking, draining off liquid fat and trying low-fat marinades to add flavor. Lean meat options are 90% lean ground beef, sirloin steak, pork loin chops, skinless baked chicken breast or ground white-meat turkey. Or try the following meat alternatives.

BEANS, LEGUMES, SEEDS & DARK GREEN VEGETABLES. Lentils, soybeans, black beans, chickpeas, peanuts, spinach and quinoa are all sources of protein and iron. At meals, pair them with vitamin C-rich foods that enhance iron absorption, such as green and red bell peppers, broccoli, Brussels sprouts, bok choy, tomatoes or tomato juice, potatoes, oranges or cantaloupe.

To create your own meatless burgers, combine beans, seeds, nuts, whole grains, onions, mushrooms or other veggies in a food processor with favorite seasonings and a binder (see "Egg & Substitutes"). Shape into burgers and grill or bake.

PORTOBELLO MUSHROOMS. Rich in flavor, portobello caps are a popular burger alternative, great for marinating and grilling or stuffing and baking. They're low-calorie and fat-free and provide protein and essential amino acids, potassium and vitamin B.

SEITAN (OR WHEAT MEAT). Seitan (say-TAHN) is made from the natural protein found in wheat and has a chewy, meat-like consistency. It has as much protein as sirloin steak per serving, has no saturated fat and is low in calories, fat, carbs and sodium when made from scratch with vital wheat gluten flour.

TEMPEH, PLAIN. Sold in flat, rectangular slabs, tempeh (TEHM-peh) is a probiotic food, high in protein and fiber and low in fat. Made from fermented soybeans, tempeh has a mild, nutty flavor and works beautifully crumbled into stir-fries or sliced, seasoned and grilled.

TEXTURED VEGETABLE PROTEIN (TVP), ORGANIC. Also sold as textured soy protein (TSP), this inexpensive meat substitute is sold in dry nuggets and reconstituted in liquid before cooking.

TOFU, ORGANIC. Soybean curds are pressed like cheese to make tofu (TOH-foo), an Asian staple. Tofu is a source of protein, calcium, iron, omega-3 fats and other minerals. The fat and nutrition content varies, so check labels. Stir-fry or marinate and grill firm tofu. Add tofu to salads or use silken tofu to make no-egg quiches and sauces. See also "Egg & Substitutes."

MILK & SUBSTITUTES – Some health advocates argue passionately for their dairy choices: whole vs. low-fat, homogenized vs. raw, organic grass-fed vs. factory-farmed. Here, we'll stick to a basic comparison of milk varieties found in your local grocery:

· WHOLE MILK has about 150 calories, 8 grams fat, 5 grams saturated fat
· REDUCED-FAT (2%) MILK has about 130 calories, 5 grams fat and 3 grams saturated fat
· LOW-FAT (1%) MILK has about 110 calories, 2.5 grams fat and 1.5 grams saturated fat
· FAT-FREE (SKIM) MILK has about 90 calories, 0 grams fat and 0 grams saturated fat

(Continued)

(*"Milk & Substitutes," continued*) Vegans and those avoiding cholesterol or lactose will find shelves filled with lactose-free and nondairy substitutes—many of them organic and fortified with calcium, iron and vitamins A and D. But shop smart and read the labels. All nondairy milk products are not low in fat or calories, and some contain added sugar, sodium and oils.

ALMOND MILK, PLAIN. Almond and other nut milks add richness to drinks and dishes and contain beneficial antioxidants. Almond Breeze® Unsweetened Almond Milk contains 40 calories, 3.5 grams of fat and 0 grams of saturated fat per cup. You can also make almond milk at home by blending 1 part presoaked raw almonds with 4 parts water and a dash of salt in a blender. Use as is or strain through cheesecloth.

COCONUT MILK, UNSWEETENED. This creamy milk, squeezed from the meat of a coconut, is equally at home in sweet and savory dishes and ideally suited to Indian and Asian recipes. Typically, coconut milk is high in calories and saturated fat. Light versions are available.

RICE MILK, PLAIN. It works well as a stand-alone drink and in cereal, smoothies and desserts. One cup has about 120 calories, 2 grams of fat and no saturated fat, but with nearly 3 times the carbs in cow's milk, it may not be a good choice for diabetics.

SOY MILK, PLAIN. Soy milk provides protein, omega-3 fats, B vitamins and iron and is low in saturated fat (about .5 gram per cup). A cup has about 100 calories and 4 grams of fat. Many brands offer reduced-fat versions. Swap equal amounts of soy for dairy milk in smoothies, soups and baked goods. NOTE: Acidic ingredients make soy milk curdle.

FEELING MORE ADVENTUROUS? Try hemp milk and oat milk!

MOLASSES - *See "Sugar & Substitutes."*

N

NATURAL GRANULATED SUGAR - *See "Sugar & Substitutes."*
NORI - It's an edible seaweed sold in dried sheets, used to wrap sushi ingredients. Find nori in Asian markets and some groceries.
NUTRITIONAL YEAST - *See "Cheese & Substitutes."*

O

OILS, FATS & SUBSTITUTES - Knowledge about the different types of oils and fats is ever evolving, but these recommendations reflect current wisdom.

REDUCE SATURATED FATS. Found in dairy and other animal products as well as in palm, palm kernel and coconut oils, saturated fats are known to raise LDL (bad) blood cholesterol. High levels of LDL are linked to an increased risk for heart disease and stroke. NOTE: Coconut oil contains a type of saturated fat believed by some to offer unique health benefits. Further research is needed to confirm or dispel that belief.

AVOID TRANS FATS. Trans fatty acids (trans fats) are found in margarine, fried foods and processed snack foods that contain partially hydrogenated oils. Like saturated fats, trans fats can raise LDL cholesterol and may also lower HDL (good) cholesterol.

LIMIT OMEGA-6S AND BOOST OMEGA-3S. Both omega-6 and omega-3 fatty acids are types of polyunsaturated fats and work together to promote health. But getting an overabundance of omega-6—found in oils such as corn and soybean—may contribute to inflammation in the body and the increased risk of chronic diseases. Intake of omega-3—from sources such as uncooked flaxseed oil, ground flaxseeds, walnuts and salmon—may help reduce inflammation. Oils high in polyunsaturated fats are less heat-stable and best used uncooked in salad dressings or dips or added to food *after* cooking to preserve nutrients and flavor.

FAVOR MONOUNSATURATED FATS. Monounsaturated fats, when used in place of other dietary fats, are linked to increasing HDL cholesterol levels and may help to slightly decrease LDL levels. Oils with an abundance of these fats, such as olive and canola, are considered more heat-stable for cooking depending on the grade of oil chosen (*see "Heating Oil," page 22*). The least refined grade of olive oil—extra-virgin—has a lower smoke point and is best cooked at lower temperatures or drizzled cold over dishes to enjoy its richer flavor and heart-healthy benefits. More refined grades—such as extra-light olive oil—have a more neutral flavor and can cook at higher temperatures. Workhorse frying oils labeled "high oleic"—such as high-oleic canola and sunflower—are bred to have a greater percentage of monounsaturated fats and fewer polyunsaturated fats to make them stable for high-heat cooking.

SEEK OUT ORGANIC. Some pesticides are fat soluble, accumulating in a plant's fatty acids and oils. Buying organic oil can limit your exposure.

WATCH FAT AND CALORIES. All oils add calories and fat. Here are a few easy methods for reducing your intake: a) Cut oil in half by mixing it with water in a spray bottle and spritzing a pan for sautéing. b) Bring a couple tablespoons of water or vinegar to a sizzle in a wok when making a stir-fry. c) Grill, broil or bake foods you would typically fry. d) Add flavor with herbs, spices and rubs instead of oils and fats. e) To lower fat and add fiber in baked dishes, substitute unsweetened, natural applesauce for oil in equal amounts.

O

OLD-FASHIONED ROLLED OATS - A whole-grain food, these oats are steamed, rolled and toasted to allow for faster cooking and a creamy consistency. Oats provide protein, iron, fiber and B vitamins and are known to improve blood sugar and cholesterol levels when eaten regularly. *See also "Steel-Cut Oats."*

P

PANKO BREADCRUMBS - Panko is a Japanese style of crunchy breadcrumb, ideal for breading meat, fish or tofu.

PICADILLO – *See page 74.*
POBLANO CHILE PEPPER – Poblano *(poh-BLAH-noh)* chiles start out green with mild heat and get hotter as they ripen to a deep reddish-black. Dried poblanos are called ancho chiles.

Q
QUINOA – Usually thought of as a whole grain, quinoa *(KEEN-wah)* is actually a seed. One cup of cooked quinoa has 60% more protein, 25% more fiber and 15% fewer carbohydrates than a cup of cooked brown rice. It's also gluten- and cholesterol-free and offers all nine essential amino acids.

R
RED CHILE PEPPER – Different types of chiles are labeled "red chile" in supermarkets, and their heat can vary. Fresh cayenne chiles work well in any of the recipes that call for red chiles, but feel free to experiment with other types found in your market.

S
SALSA LIZANO – *See page 74.*
SALT & SUBSTITUTES – Salt (sodium chloride) helps balance fluids, electrolytes and pH levels, is essential to muscle function and plays a role in digestion. But with high amounts of sodium in many canned and processed foods, some of us get far more than we need, which may increase the risk for hypertension and heart disease. Check labels and cook more meals from scratch to control the amount of sodium in your food. Rinse canned beans. Reduce reliance on salt by using high-flavor, low-sodium ingredients that awaken the senses—basil, rosemary, cumin, garlic and onion powders, herb vinegars, citrus juices, grated ginger, crushed red pepper, Tabasco® and Mrs. Dash® salt-free seasoning blends. Marinate foods to infuse more flavor in dishes.
SOUR CREAM & SUBSTITUTES – Sour cream is cream fermented with lactic-acid bacteria to make it thick and slightly tart. To reduce calories and fat, try light sour cream or replace with reduced-fat Greek yogurt, which offers more protein, fewer carbs and less cholesterol and saturated fat than sour cream. Commercial vegan brands taste like the real thing but may have more additives or hydrogenated oils than you want. Recipes can be found online to create nondairy, cholesterol-free versions using organic silken tofu.
STEEL-CUT OATS – Chewier than rolled oats with a slightly nutty flavor, steel-cut oats undergo less processing and require more time to cook. *See also "Old-Fashioned Rolled Oats."*
STEVIA – *See "Sugar & Substitutes."*
SUGAR & SUBSTITUTES – Total all the natural and added sugars in foods and you see how easy it is to max out your daily intake. Bottom line: Sugar is sugar—high in calories with little to no nutritional value—so save those empty calories for occasional treats. Following are sweeteners used in this book, along with substitutes to suit individual needs.

AGAVE NECTAR, ORGANIC. Derived from a desert succulent plant, this vegan syrup is an alternative to sugar or honey. While lower than white sugar on the glycemic index, agave *(ah-GAH-veh)* is not lower in calories or carbs. Some brands have added corn syrup and as much as 90% fructose, known to raise triglycerides and the risk for heart disease, so be picky! Find "raw," organic, pure agave with less than 55% fructose online or in some natural-foods markets. In baking recipes, substitute ⅔ cup agave for each cup of granulated sugar. Reduce other liquids in the recipe by 20% of the measure of agave used and lower oven temperature by 25°. Replace honey with agave nectar in equal amounts—no other recipe adjustments needed.

BROWN SUGAR. Commercial brown sugar is refined white sugar with molasses added. Light brown sugar has a delicate flavor while dark brown sugar has more molasses and a more intense flavor. Both are good for baking when that flavor is desired, but neither is an ideal substitute for white sugar.

DATE SUGAR. One of the few nutrient-rich sweeteners, date sugar is a whole food made from ground, dehydrated dates and is high in fiber, vitamins and minerals. In recipes that don't require sugar to be dissolved, date sugar can be substituted in equal amounts for granulated sugar. Or blend ripe dates with water to make date paste *(see "Great Dates," page 116)*, a substitute for agave nectar or honey.

FRUIT JUICE CONCENTRATE. Replace sugar with naturally sweet or unsweetened fruit juice concentrate. Orange, mango, pineapple, peach, pear and guava juices are frequently used to replace table sugar in beverages or to add slight sweetness to marinades. For baking, replace 1 cup white sugar with ⅔ cup concentrate thawed to room temperature. Reduce total liquids in the recipe by ⅓ cup for each cup of fruit juice used and reduce oven temperature by 25°. When baking with acidic juices, add ¼ teaspoon baking soda per cup of fruit sweetener.

HONEY. Honey has more calories and carbs than granulated sugar, but it's sweeter so you can use less. Raw honey offers enzymes, minerals, vitamins and phytonutrients. Heating can destroy these nutrients, so some bakers opt for lower-cost pasteurized (pure) honey for baking. Substitute ¾ cup + 1 tablespoon of honey for each cup of white sugar. Reduce total liquids by ¼ cup and lower oven temperature by 25°. **NOTE:** Honey can carry a bacteria that is harmful to infants under 12 months.

MAPLE SYRUP, ORGANIC. Maple syrup is rich in flavor and lower than sugar on the glycemic index. Skip imitations with corn syrup and maple flavoring and find naturally processed syrup in natural-foods markets. Use ¾ cup for every cup of white sugar and decrease total liquids in the recipe by 3 tablespoons.

MOLASSES. Light, dark and blackstrap molasses are all byproducts of the sugar refining process and retain some of the nutrients white sugar loses. Blackstrap molasses is a robust, slightly bitter syrup containing the richest concentration of minerals, including iron, calcium, magnesium and *(Continued)*

("Sugar & Substitutes," continued) potassium. In some baking recipes, you can replace up to half the white sugar with molasses. Swap 1 cup of sugar for 1⅓ cups of molasses and reduce the amount of total liquids in the recipe by 5 tablespoons for each cup of white sugar replaced. Then add ½ teaspoon baking soda per cup of molasses used. (Whew! Got all that?)

NATURAL GRANULATED SUGAR (OR EVAPORATED CANE JUICE). Milled cane sugars, such as Florida Crystals® Natural Cane Sugar, are less processed than refined white sugar and retain trace amounts of nutrients. Use 1 to 1 in place of refined white sugar.

STEVIA. A no-calorie, refined herbal sweetener, stevia (STEE-vee-uh) is sold in dry or liquid form. Its sweetness is typically much higher than table sugar but differs from brand to brand. Start by replacing each cup of sugar in a recipe with 1 teaspoon of stevia and adjust to taste. Or try a product specially formulated for baking (see page 119). Stevia is fine for baking below 400°.

TURBINADO SUGAR (OR RAW SUGAR). Coarse, golden brown turbinado (ter-bin-AH-doh) sugar is from the first pressing of the sugar cane and retains some nutrients. It's a more natural replacement for refined white sugar and can be substituted in equal amounts; however, turbinado may not be appropriate for some complex baking recipes that call for fine or granulated sugar.

WHITE SUGAR (OR TABLE SUGAR OR SUCROSE). Raw sugar from sugar cane or beets is refined to produce white granulated sugar, eliminating all vitamins and minerals.

CUTTING BACK ON SUGAR? Try starting with half the sweetener called for in recipes and adjust to taste. Experiment with cinnamon, cardamom, nutmeg, ginger or mace to enhance the sweet flavors in foods.

T

TAHINI – Tahini (tah-HEE-nee) is a paste made from ground sesame seeds and is used in Middle Eastern dishes such as hummus.

TEMPEH – See "Meat & Substitutes."

THICKENERS – AGAR-AGAR POWDER. Made from seaweed, vegan agar-agar (AY-gar AY-gar)—also called kanten—can replace nonvegan gelatin in equal amounts to thicken or gel puddings, custards and sauces. Found in Asian and natural-foods markets, agar-agar is high in fiber and a source of iron and calcium, with no fat or carbohydrates. It sets more quickly than gelatin.

ARROWROOT POWDER. Made from the rootstalks of the arrowroot tuber, this powder can replace flour or cornstarch to thicken condiments and fruit-based dessert sauces with pleasing clarity. Low-cal, high in calcium and gluten-free, it can substitute for wheat flour if you have a gluten sensitivity. Dishes made with arrowroot freeze and thaw without losing integrity and handle acidity well. It's not ideal for dairy-based or meat sauces, though. Replace 1 tablespoon cornstarch with 2¼ teaspoons arrowroot powder. Adjust the amount if needed. Stir into a little cold water.

CORNSTARCH. High in calories and carbohydrates, cornstarch is a dense powder most often used as a (Continued page 152)

GLOSSARY & SUBSTITUTIONS (CONTINUED)

("*Thickeners,*" continued)   thickener in puddings, sauces and soups.

KUDZU (OR KUZU). A chalklike vine vilified as a weed in the southern U.S., kudzu (*KOOHD-zoo*) is considered a health supplement by its fans, with antioxidants and heart-healthy isoflavones. Buy kudzu in chunks, then crush and dissolve it in cold liquid before introducing it to something hot. Substitute an equal amount of kudzu powder for cornstarch to thicken soups, sauces, gravies and puddings. Unlike arrowroot powder, kudzu continues to thicken even as the dish cools. NOTE: Kudzu may not be advised for those taking hormones or antidiabetic or anticoagulant drugs. Consult your doctor.

TZATZIKI SAUCE – Tzatziki (*dza-DZEE-kee*) is a traditional Greek white sauce made with strained yogurt and typically includes cucumber, garlic and dill or parsley.

V

VEGAN – A vegan (*VEE-gun*) eschews all animal products—including meat, dairy, eggs and gelatin—and certain brands of wine, beer, sugar and other foods processed or fortified with animal byproducts.

VEGETARIAN, OVO-LACTO – An ovo-lacto vegetarian may choose to eat dairy and eggs but typically avoids all meat and byproducts from animal slaughter, such as chicken stock, fish sauce and rennet, found in some cheeses. NOTE: The recipes labeled as vegetarian in this book do not distinguish between cheeses made with or without rennet. For this information, consult product manufacturers or articles at vrg.org.

W

WHOLE GRAINS – Grains are important sources of B vitamins, folate, iron and other essential minerals. Whole grains—such as brown rice, whole oats and whole wheat—retain the entire kernel, which contains nutrients and fiber that are stripped away in refined grains. When refined grains are enriched, the fiber and many nutrients are not added back in. *See also "Dietary Fiber."*

Y

YOGURT, PLAIN – Yogurt offers protein, calcium and B vitamins. Go for brands with live, active cultures, known as probiotics, which aid with digestion. *See also "Greek Yogurt."*

YUCA ROOT (OR CASSAVA) – See page 111.

— *Researched and written by Ashley Pound with contributions from Janine M. Koutsky, MS, and reviewed by Molly Morgan, RD, CDN, CSSD*

METRIC CONVERSIONS

The recipes in this book have not been tested using metric measurements. Some variations in quality may occur when converting. Keep in mind that the weight of dry ingredients varies according the volume or density of each. Weigh dry ingredients using a metric scale.

METRIC CONVERSION CALCULATIONS (*for precise measurements*)

fluid ounces x 29.57 = grams	pounds x 0.45 = kilograms
ounces (dry) x 28.35 = grams	cups x 0.24 = liters
pounds x 453.6 = grams	Fahrenheit – 32 ÷ 1.8 = Celsius

VOLUME (LIQUID) APPROXIMATE MEASUREMENTS

1 teaspoon = ⅙ fluid ounce = 5 milliliters
1 tablespoon = ½ fluid ounce = 15 milliliters
2 tablespoons = 1 fluid ounce = ⅛ cup = 30 milliliters
¼ cup = 2 fluid ounces = 60 milliliters
⅓ cup = 2⅔ fluid ounces = 80 milliliters
½ cup = 4 fluid ounces = 120 milliliters
1 cup = ½ pint = 8 fluid ounces = 250 milliliters
2 cups = 1 pint = 16 fluid ounces = 500 milliliters
4 cups = 1 quart = 1 liter

WEIGHT (MASS) APPROX. MEASUREMENTS

1 ounce = 28 grams
2 ounces = 57 grams
4 ounces = ¼ pound = 113 grams
8 ounces = ½ pound = 230 grams
12 ounces = ¾ pound = 340 grams
16 ounces = 1 pound = 450 grams

OVEN APPROXIMATE TEMPERATURES
FAHRENHEIT (F) TO CELSIUS (C)

250°F = 120°C = very low/slow
300°F = 150°C = low/slow
350°F = 175°C = medium/moderate
400°F = 205°C = hot/quick
450°F = 230°C = very hot

VOLUME (DRY) APPROX. MEASUREMENTS

¼ teaspoon = 1 milliliter
½ teaspoon = 2 milliliters
¾ teaspoon = 4 milliliters
1 teaspoon = 5 milliliters
1 tablespoon = 15 milliliters
¼ cup = 59 milliliters
⅓ cup = 79 milliliters
½ cup = 118 milliliters
⅔ cup = 158 milliliters
¾ cup = 177 milliliters
1 cup = 225 milliliters

HELPFUL TOOLS FOR CALCULATING CONVERSIONS & SUBSTITUTIONS (*accessed Sept. 12, 2012; slight variations occur from site to site*)

CONVERSION CALCULATORS - dianasdesserts.com/index.cfm/
    fuseaction/tools.measures/Measures.cfm
COOK'S TOOLS - southernfood.about.com/library/info/blcooks.htm
MARYLAND METRICS - mdmetric.com/tech/kitchen.htm

ONLINE COOKING CONVERTER - convert-me.com/en/convert/cooking
THE METRIC KITCHEN - jsward.com/cooking/index.shtml
USDA MEASUREMENT CONVERSION TABLES - ars.usda.gov/Aboutus/
    docs.htm?docid=9617

SOURCES

"Antioxidants and Your Immune System: Super Foods for Optimal Health." WebMD.com, accessed Sept. 12, 2012, webmd.com/a-to-z-guides/antioxidants-your-immune-system-super-foods-optimal-health.

Armstrong, Cheryl H. "Top 20 Healthy Recipe Ingredient Substitutions." Nutrition and Food Safety Workshop for Quantity Food Providers, Apr. 27, 1999; accessed Feb. 24, 2012, cfs.purdue.edu/extension/pdf/recipesubst.pdf.

"Baking with Sugar and Sugar Substitutes." AllRecipes.com, accessed Apr. 22, 2012, allrecipes.com/howto/baking-with-sugar-and-sugar-substitutes.

"Balsamic Vinegar." CooksIllustrated.com, March 1, 2007; accessed Sept. 10, 2012, cooksillustrated.com/tastetests/overview.asp?docid=10133.

Bauer, Joy. "Salt Substitutes: Are They Safe?" JoyBauer.com, accessed Nov. 1, 2012, joybauer.com/high-blood-pressure/salt-substitutes.aspx.

Bellatti, Andy and Andrew Wilder. "The Handy Dandy Cooking Oil Comparison Chart." SmallBites.com, Feb. 13, 2012; accessed Feb. 20, 2012, smallbites.andybellatti.com/handy-dandy-cooking-oil-comparison-chart.

"Blackstrap Molasses." The World's Healthiest Foods, accessed Apr. 22, 2012, whfoods.com/genpage.php?tname=foodspice&dbid=118.

Choudhury, Ankana Dey. "Cornstarch Substitutes." Buzzle, updated Jan. 11, 2012; accessed Apr. 20, 2012, buzzle.com/articles/cornstarch-substitute.html.

"Common Misconceptions about Cholesterol." American Heart Association, updated Nov. 16, 2011; accessed May 12, 2012, heart.org/HEARTORG/Conditions/Cholesterol/PreventionTreatmentofHighCholesterol/Common-Misconceptions-about-Cholesterol_UCM_305638_Article.jsp.

"Cooking Oils." Whole Foods, accessed Sept. 12, 2012, wholefoodsmarket.com/recipes/food-guides/cooking-oils.

"Curry Powder." AllRecipes.com, accessed Sept. 12, 2012, http://allrecipes.com/howto/curry-powder.

"Dietary Supplement Fact Sheet: Iron." Office of Dietary Supplements, National Institutes of Health, accessed Sept. 13, 2012, ods.od.nih.gov/factsheets/Iron-HealthProfessional.

Edgar, Julie. "Medicinal Uses of Honey," reviewed Dec. 11, 2011; accessed Oct. 28, 2012, webmd.com/diet/features/medicinal-uses-of-honey.

"Eggs." The Cook's Thesaurus, accessed Sept. 12, 2012, foodsubs.com/eggs.html.

Ehrlich, Steven D. "Green Tea." University of Maryland Medical Center, 2011; accessed Aug. 20, 2012, umm.edu/altmed/articles/green-tea-000255.htm.

Geiger, Brian. "Baking Soda and Baking Powder." FineCooking.com, Oct. 28, 2009; accessed May 11, 2012, finecooking.com/item/12173/baking-soda-and-baking-powder.

Gregor, Michael. "The Healthiest Sweetener." NutritionFacts.org, Nov. 8, 2010; accessed Apr. 20, 2012, nutritionfacts.org/video/the-healthiest-sweetener.

Hackett, Jolinda. "What is Quinoa?" About.com, accessed Sept. 12, 2012, vegetarian.about.com/od/glossary/g/whatisquinoa.htm.

"Health Studies on Whole Grains." Whole Grains Council, accessed Sept. 12, 2012, wholegrainscouncil.org/whole-grains-101/health-studies-on-whole-grains.

Herbst, Sharon Tyler and Ron Herbst. *The New Food Lover's Companion,* 4th ed. New York: Barron's Educational Series, 2007. IPad edition.

"Know Your Fats." American Heart Association, updated June 25, 2012, heart.org/HEARTORG/Conditions/Cholesterol/PreventionTreatmentofHighCholesterol/Know-Your-Fats_UCM_305628_Article.jsp.

"Liquid Sweeteners." The Cook's Thesaurus, accessed Apr. 21, 2012, foodsubs.com/syrups.html.

Mayo Clinic Staff. "Dietary Fiber: Essential for a Healthy Diet." MayoClinic.com, accessed Sept. 12, 2012, mayoclinic.com/health/fiber/NU00033.

"Milk vs. Rice Milk." FitDay.com, accessed Sept. 14, 2012, fitday.com/fitness-articles/nutrition/healthy-eating/milk-vs-rice-milk.html#b.

Myklebust, Monica and Jenna Wunder. "Healing Foods Pyramid." University of Michigan Health System, 2010; accessed Sept. 14, 2012, med.umich.edu/umim/food-pyramid/fats.htm.

"Sugar to Agave Conversion." GlutenFreeHelp.info, Jan. 21, 2010; accessed Apr. 14, 2012, glutenfreehelp.info/helpful-information/sugar-to-agave-conversion.

"Sugars." The Cook's Thesaurus, accessed Sept. 12, 2012, foodsubs.com/sweeten.html.

"The Great Organic Agave Nectar Controversy..." confabulicious.com, May 31, 2010; accessed Apr. 20, 2012, confabulicious.com/the-great-agave-controversy-to-use-or-not-to-use-that-is-the-question.

"The Nutrition of Agar." FitDay.com, accessed Sept. 13, 2012, fitday.com/fitness-articles/nutrition/healthy-eating/the-nutrition-of-agar.html#b.

"Vegetarian Nutrition." The Vegetarian Resource Group, accessed Feb. 20, 2012, vrg.org/nutrition.

Ward, Elizabeth M. "Cholesterol and Cooking: Fats and Oils." WebMD.com, accessed Sept. 14, 2012, webmd.com/cholesterol-management/features/cholesterol-and-cooking-fats-and-oils.

Wood, Rebecca. "Making the 'Gravy.'" The Humane Society, Jan. 19, 2010; accessed Sept. 12, 2012, humanesociety.org/issues/eating/recipes/techniques/slurry.html.

Zeratsky, Katherine. "Can Coconut Oil Help Me Lose Weight?" MayoClinic.com, accessed Aug. 15, 2012, mayoclinic.com/health/coconut-oil-and-weight-loss/AN01899.

Brand-specific nutrition facts and substitution formulas were gathered from manufacturers' websites. Other substitutions were provided by the editor or consultants or adapted from the above sources. Results may vary.

PROP CREDITS

pages 2-3
Gray stone bowl by **ABC Homes**; turquoise dish, green dish by **Jono Pandolfi**

page 25
White and silver luster bowl by **ABC Homes**

pages 30-31
Round ceramic ivory plates, brown and white ceramic cups by **Jono Pandolfi**

page 41
Ivory ceramic plates by **Jono Pandolfi**

page 44
Place mat, salad spoon/fork set by **ABC Homes**; green plate, dressing cup by **Jono Pandolfi**

pages 50-51
Small rustic blue bowls by **ABC Homes**

page 64
Marine blue nettle liner by **ABC Homes**

pages 66-67
Charcoal hemp place mat by **ABC Homes**; white ceramic plate by **Jono Pandolfi**

page 101
Gray stone bowl, white bowl, place mat by **ABC Homes**; turquoise dish by **Jono Pandolfi**

page 109
Blue-green plate, bowl by **Jono Pandolfi**

pages 110-111
White ceramic bowl, dish by **Jono Pandolfi**

pages 120-121
Ivory ceramic plates by **Jono Pandolfi**

pages 138-139
Plates, cup by **Jono Pandolfi**

pages 158-159
Gray stone bowl by **ABC Homes**; turquoise dish, green dish by **Jono Pandolfi**

INDEX

INDEX (CONTINUED)